SH 2

SH 2

Everything Your Heirs Need To Know About You

Everything Your Heirs Need To Know About You

YOUR ASSETS, FAMILY HISTORY AND FINAL WISHES

David S. Magee

GRAMERCY PUBLISHING COMPANY
New York

To Dorothy
and our heirs
with love

ACKNOWLEDGMENTS

My entire family has continually encouraged this project and has assisted in the preparation of this book. I gratefully thank my wife, Dorothy, for all of her help and assistance in discussing, planning and typing the manuscript. My son and daughters, and their husbands, have given excellent suggestions which I have used. My thanks to them—Sandy and Tom Burr, Pat and Rick Yuille, Judy and Richard Dugan and Dave Magee, Jr. (A special thanks to Judy, whose first-published book ignited the spark for this one.) Herbert A. Milliken, Jr., Howard L. Gay and John W. Olson were kind enough to take their valuable time to read the manuscript and constructively criticize it. My thanks to Maryann Murphy for allowing the use of her graphics studio in the book's production. Thanks also to Sally Jaeger, Shelly Lowenkopf, Jody Joseph and many good friends who have offered valuable suggestions and support. Finally, for time spent far and beyond the call of friendship, I thank Dr. Richard L. Rapport, M.D., for his enthusiastic encouragement and for the many hours he spent editing the manuscript.

Designer & Editor:
J. Magee Dugan

This 1987 edition is published by Gramercy Publishing Company, distributed by Crown Publishers, Inc., 225 Park Avenue South, New York, New York 10003, by arrangement with La Madre Distributors.

Manufactured in the United States of America

Library of Congress Cataloging-in-Publication Data

Magee, David S.
Everything your heirs need to know about you.

1. Estate planning—United States—Miscellanea.
I. Title.
KF750.Z9M26   1987   346.7305′2   87-8575
                ISBN 0-517-64368-5   347.30652

ISBN 0-517-64368-5
h g f e d c b a

CONTENTS

Topics discussed at the beginning of each chapter are noted in italics, followed by forms designed for your personal use.

INTRODUCTION

It is easy to estimate that over a billion dollars now held in stocks, bonds, insurance, bank accounts and other assets around the country will never be claimed by the rightful owners. New York State alone already has an unclaimed property fund that tops $500 million.

The bulk of this fortune lies unclaimed because heirs to these assets have no idea their inheritances exist. It is not lack of concern for heirs or for the destiny of personal assets that creates this growing untapped treasure. Certainly most of us would much prefer to see the fruits of our lifelong efforts benefit loved ones rather than landing in state coffers.

Why then are so many heirs unaware of property intended for them? The answer is simply that many people fail to leave their families a clear record of their assets. The widespread habit of filing important papers in shoe boxes, bottom drawers and scattered files leaves families searching months, even years, for needed papers and records — and the search will not even begin if the family does not know an asset exists.

One California family was recently tracked down by private investigators for a company that had sold stock to their father over twenty years before. Since no record of the $500 in stock was found after the father's death, the family was not aware of his investment. Thanks to the company's president, who had personally sold the stock to their father and hired the investigators, the heirs were located just one week before the State was to claim the assets. The $500 in stock? It is now worth $160,000. This family was fortunate: Most heirs to unrecorded assets never know their inheritances exist.

Comedian W. C. Fields was an extreme case. Memories of his impoverished youth brought Fields recurring nightmares about being stranded in a strange city without funds. The wealthy performer recalled opening as many as 700 bank accounts, often in fictitious names, in the cities he visited around the world. Fields left no record for his heirs and only 48 of his bank accounts were located after his death. Over a million dollars of his estate is thought to have remained scattered in hundreds of undiscovered bank accounts.

While few of us have 700 bank accounts (much less the million to put in them), we may have picked up a couple of life insurance policies, bought a few shares of stock or opened an extra savings account or two over the years. We also can probably locate the papers to prove it, perhaps with a little digging. The question is whether anyone else can.

A will that fully outlines assets is all that is needed then, right? Not true. In the first place, few people update their wills with each acquisition or sale of personal property. Also, wills often simply divide estates into bulk portions, mentioning major assets and leaving heirs, executors and the courts to determine the remaining contents of the estate. Without clear records, the family is faced with the burdensome and often costly task of locating records, papers and documents to establish the extent of the estate.

Certain major assets are not even typically included in wills. Life insurance proceeds, pensions, Social Security and veteran's benefits all have fixed plans of distribution unaffected by wills, and so they are not commonly mentioned. A clear, up-to-date listing of available assets and benefits can prove invaluable to your heirs. This book is designed to make that easy to provide.

Also of value to the family is a record of personal wishes regarding funeral and burial arrangements. Many people live together for fifty years without discussing their wishes. Without intent, they leave many distressing decisions for their loved ones. You can spare your family this distress by simply deciding upon and recording your own preferences. A will, however, is not the best place for detailing final arrangements, since wills are often read after the burial. This book discusses various arrangements that can be made and provides a place to express your wishes.

Perhaps the most cherished legacy you can provide your heirs is your unique knowledge of family history, your recollections about your own life, interests and accomplishments, and other special remembrances. These can be shared in the first section of the book.

At the end of the book, you will find lists of papers and documents that should be readily available to your heirs. By gathering these papers and the facts suggested on the pages that follow, you will be able to organize your affairs and provide an invaluable guide for your heirs.

A GUIDE TO THIS BOOK

The first part of each chapter contains information for you and your heirs. This is followed by forms designed for you to provide your heirs with a detailed personal record of your assets, family history, final wishes and other notes for your heirs.

The Document Check Lists at the end of the book provide an outline for the collection of birth certificates, marriage certificates, funeral pre-arrangement agreements and other papers that will be of value to your heirs. Any original documents that are irreplaceable or have intrinsic value (stock certificates, bonds, etc.) should be kept in a safe-deposit box, with copies in your personal files.

There is no need to complete the forms in the order in which they appear. It may be more enjoyable to go through a first time jotting down information which is readily available. Then you may go back and fill in the missing pieces.

You may find forms which do not apply to you. If so, mark them "N.A." (not applicable) and go on. *If the forms do apply to you, fill them in.* Even though you may not have all of the answers at first, take the time to find them. You know the sources; your heirs may not.

Fill in the forms with a soft lead pencil. If your decisions change as time goes by, it will be easy to erase what you have previously written and insert new directions for your heirs. Or, if you prefer ink, correct with typewriter correction fluid.

Print legibly. After all, if you take the time to organize this record for your heirs, you want them to be able to read it.

Keep the forms up-to-date. As changes occur, update the forms. It is a good plan to review them at least once a year.

Discuss this book with your heirs. They must be aware of its existence, know where it is located and know what it says in order for it to be of value to them. Although for many people death is a difficult subject to discuss, this feeling should be overcome. Sit down and have a frank and open talk with those closest to you.

It is unlikely that you will be able to complete this guide in one or two sittings. Some information will take extra thought or research. But don't look upon it as a task. If you approach it in manageable sections and look upon it as a fascinating family project, you will find it can give you great satisfaction to track down bits and pieces of your family history, locate the missing birth certificate and gradually put your affairs in order. These records can be of great interest and value to you during your lifetime. But the greatest satisfaction will be in knowing that should anything happen to you, your loved ones will have your notes, your wishes and the information that you have provided to guide them.

❖❖❖❖❖

TO YOUR HEIRS:

A "Guide for Survivors" can be found in Chapter 9. This provides a list of steps to be taken at a time of family loss with references to appropriate pages in this book.

Everything Your Heirs Need To Know About You

There is no one who knows your personal history as well as you. Do your children know where you were born? Where you went to school? In what cities you have lived? Your mother's family name? Where your parents lived or are buried? The different types of work experiences you have had? The hobbies and clubs you have enjoyed through the years? Probably not.

And yet, haven't you asked yourself many of these questions in regard to your own parents? Or your grandparents? Or your brothers and sisters? Most of us become more interested in family history as we age. If someone does not record the facts, they will be lost. *You* are the one who can do this best.

Go through the forms in Chapter 1 and fill in the answers that you know. There will be many blanks when you finish. Make the gathering of the rest of the answers an enjoyable project. Telephone or drop a note to a parent, brother, sister, aunt, uncle, son or daughter and gradually complete your personal history. As a bonus, you may rekindle family ties.

GENERAL OUTLINE

The forms in Chapter 1 are set out in the following order:

General Summary
Marital Background
Children
Father
Mother
Grandparents
Brothers & Sisters
Educational Background
Organizations, Unions, Clubs, etc.
Work Background
Religion, Politics and Hobbies
Places of Residence
Miscellaneous

The form entitled "General Summary" provides a place for you to record pertinent facts of your life.

Forms are provided for three spouses, six children and five siblings. If needed, you may photocopy extra forms and keep them in your personal files. Keep in mind that forms not applicable to your present situation may become useful because families change in unforeseen ways as a result of births, deaths, divorces and marriages.

Many of the forms have space provided on the back where you may write personal notes about your relatives. You may choose to give a brief history, to discuss their beliefs or accomplishments, or to share personal reminiscences. Use the space as you wish.

The remaining forms in Chapter 1 seek more detailed information about you — your educational background, where you have worked and lived, organizations you have joined, your religion, politics and hobbies.

Finally, you will find a section entitled "Miscellaneous." This is for *you* to fill in with personal notes about yourself or your family — your interests, accomplishments, thoughts or desires. Add anything you consider to be of interest to your family and heirs. Don't be modest! If you did something in your lifetime of which you are proud, tell them about it. They will be proud, too. If something very humorous happened to you, your heirs will enjoy it. Remember how you were fascinated with the interesting stories told to you by your mother, father and grandparents? Your heirs are just as interested in your remembrances.

A primary purpose of the forms in Chapter 1 is to provide enjoyment for your heirs. However, there are other purposes. At the time of death, some of this information will be used in the preparation of a death certificate, newspaper obituary, Federal Estate Tax Return, State Inheritance Tax Return, Income Tax Return and many other administrative forms.

BIRTH AND MARRIAGE CERTIFICATES

The vast majority of births, deaths and marriages are reported to the proper authorities so that a lasting record can be maintained. There are a number of reasons, however, why it may be difficult to obtain records when they are needed. In the not too distant past, many births occurred in private homes and went unreported. Occasionally, courthouses or other record depositories were destroyed by fire. Records escaping this fate may be incorrect because of typographical errors, misunderstanding of names and other errors which are bound to occur.

There may be a long delay after a request for copies of certificates while records are corrected or re-established. It is a good idea to request them now so they will always be on hand.

It is suggested that you have in your possession two *certified* copies each of your birth certificate, your spouse's birth certificate, your marriage certificate, and the birth certificates of your dependent children.

Each State has its own method of maintaining these records. They can usually be obtained from the County Clerk, Registrar or Recorder of the county in which the birth or marriage took place. Many States have a central clearing house for this at the state capital, generally called the State Department of Vital Statistics.

There is no standard fee for providing these records. Fees generally range from two to five dollars. Additional copies may be available at reduced rates.

To expedite the sometimes lengthy procedure of obtaining records, first inquire about the price for copies of specific certificates. Include a self-addressed, stamped envelope with your price request. Once you know the price, you can write for the copies you need, enclosing the necessary payment. Use a money order or bank check, rather than your personal check, for prompt service.

Many States will not issue copies of birth or marriage certificates unless the requestor is closely related to the person named in the certificate. It is important to identify yourself as spouse, mother or father.

DECREES AND JUDGMENTS OF DIVORCE AND ANNULMENT

It may be necessary for you to have certified copies of judgments of divorce or annulment for Social Security benefits, Veteran benefits and private pension plans. These may be obtained from the Clerk or Registrar of the Court which granted the divorce or annulment. Once again, the fee for obtaining copies will vary among the States and may depend upon the number of pages in the document.

Write a letter to the Court which granted the decree or judgment to inquire about the cost of obtaining a copy of the document. Note the date and year the divorce was granted and be sure to enclose a self-addressed, stamped envelope.

GENERAL SUMMARY

My Personal History

My full name at present: _____
First   Middle   Last

My full name at birth: _____
First   Middle   Last

Place of birth: _____
City   County   State   Country

Date of birth: _____ Soc. Sec. # _____

My present address: _____
Street Address and Apartment Number

_____
City

_____
State   Zip Code

Year residence established in this state: _____ this community: _____

My usual occupation: _____ Industry: _____

I am a citizen of _____ □ by birth; or, □ by naturalization.

I was naturalized on: _____ at _____
Date   Place

Naturalization #: _____

My naturalization papers are located: _____

Military veteran: □ Yes □ No.   Branch of Service: _____

Dates of Service: _____ Serial #: _____ Final Rank: _____

Marital status: □ Never married;   □ Married;   □ Divorced;   □ Widowed.

A certified copy of my birth and/or adoption certificate is located: _____

_____

My legal name was changed to: _____
First   Middle   Last

on_____ by _____
Date   Name of Court

located at _____
City   State

A certificate of my legal name change is located: _____

GENERAL SUMMARY

My Personal History

MARRIAGES
Sp - Spouse

	Full Name of Spouse at Birth	Last Name at Present or at Death	Date of Birth	Death
Sp #1				
Sp #2				
Sp #3				

(See pages 6-12 for further information about my spouses.)

CHILDREN
Ch - Child

	Full name of Child at Birth	Last Name at Present or at Death	Date of Birth	Death
Ch #1				
Ch #2				
Ch #3				
Ch #4				
Ch #5				
Ch #6				

(See pages 13-36 for further information about my children.)

BROTHERS & SISTERS (Siblings)
Si - Sibling

	Full Name of Brother or Sister at Birth	Last Name at Present or at Death	Date of Birth	Death
Si #1				
Si #2				
Si #3				
Si #4				
Si #5				

(See pages 45-54 for further information about my brothers and sisters.)

My Personal History

☐   I have never been married.

☐   I have been married _____ time(s) during my life.

Sp - Spouse

	Name of Spouse (before marriage)	Date of Marriage	Place of Marriage
Sp #1			
Sp #2			
Sp #3			

	Number of Children	Date Marriage Ended by Death	Divorce	Place Marriage Ended
Sp #1				
Sp #2				
Sp #3				

I have in my possession certified copies of the following documents:

	Marriage Certificate Yes	No	Divorce Decree Yes	No	Death Certificate Yes	No
Sp #1						
Sp #2						
Sp #3						

The above legal documents are located:

_____

_____

_____

My Personal History

Full name at birth: _____
                 First   *Middle*   *Last*

Place of birth: _____
           City   *County*   *State*   *Country*

Date of birth: _____ Soc. Sec. # _____

Date of marriage: _____ Place of marriage: _____

Present name: _____

Present address: _____
           Street Address and Apartment Number

_____
           City

_____
           State   *Zip Code*

Date of death: _____ Cause of death: _____

My first spouse is buried at _____
           Name of Cemetery

_____
           City   *State*

in Cemetery Lot # _____

Or: My first spouse was cremated and the ashes were _____

_____

Or: My first spouse donated his/her body to _____
                                         Name of Medical School

My first spouse and I were divorced on _____ at _____
                                          Date   *City*   *State*

We had the following children:

	Date of Birth	Full Name at Birth	Present Last Name
1st			
2nd			
3rd			
4th			
5th			
6th			

My Personal History

_____

_____

_____

_____

_____

_____

_____

_____

_____

_____

_____

_____

_____

_____

_____

_____

_____

_____

_____

_____

_____

_____

_____

_____

My Personal History

Full name at birth: _____

First   *Middle*   *Last*

Place of birth: _____

City   *County*   *State*   *Country*

Date of birth: _____ Soc. Sec. # _____

Date of marriage: _____ Place of marriage: _____

Present name: _____

Present address: _____

Street Address and Apartment Number

_____

City

_____

State   *Zip Code*

Date of death: _____ Cause of death: _____

My second spouse is buried at _____

Name of Cemetery

_____

City   *State*

in Cemetery Lot # _____

Or: My second spouse was cremated and the ashes were _____

_____

Or: My second spouse donated his/her body to _____

Name of Medical School

My second spouse and I were divorced on _____ at _____

Date   *City*   *State*

We had the following children:

	Date of Birth	Full Name at Birth	Present Last Name
1st			
2nd			
3rd			
4th			
5th			
6th			

My Personal History

_____

_____

_____

_____

_____

_____

_____

_____

_____

_____

_____

_____

_____

_____

_____

_____

_____

_____

_____

_____

_____

_____

_____

_____

_____

_____

_____

MARITAL BACKGROUND

My Personal History

Full name at birth: _____
First   Middle   Last

Place of birth: _____
City   County   State   Country

Date of birth: _____ Soc. Sec. # _____

Date of marriage: _____ Place of marriage: _____

Present name: _____

Present address: _____
Street Address and Apartment Number

_____
City

_____
State   Zip Code

Date of death: _____ Cause of death: _____

My third spouse is buried at_____
Name of Cemetery

_____
City   State

in Cemetery Lot #_____

Or: My third spouse was cremated and the ashes were _____

_____

Or: My third spouse donated his/her body to _____
Name of Medical School

My third spouse and I were divorced on _____ at _____
Date   City   State

We had the following children:

	Date of Birth	Full Name at Birth	Present Last Name
1st			
2nd			
3rd			
4th			
5th			
6th			

My Personal History

_____
_____
_____
_____
_____
_____
_____
_____
_____
_____
_____
_____
_____
_____
_____
_____
_____
_____
_____
_____
_____
_____
_____
_____
_____
_____
_____

My Personal History

Child's full name at present: _____
First   *First*   *Middle*   *Last*

Child's full name at birth: _____
First   *Middle*   *Last*

Date of birth: _____ Place of birth: _____

Adopted?_____ (If so, give details on reverse.)

Present address: _____
Street Address and Apartment Number

_____
City

_____
State   *Zip Code*

Date of death: _____ Cause of death: _____

Child is buried at _____
Name of Cemetery

_____
City   *State*

      in Cemetery Lot #_____

Or: Child was cremated and the ashes were _____

_____

Or: Child donated body to _____
Name of Medical School

☐   Child has never married.

☐   Child has been married _____ times. The names of the child's spouses, marriage dates, etc., are as follows:

	Name of Spouse (before marriage)	Birth Date	Date of Marriage	Date of Death	Divorce
#1					
#2					
#3					

My Personal History

_____

_____

_____

_____

_____

_____

_____

_____

_____

_____

_____

_____

_____

_____

_____

_____

_____

_____

_____

_____

_____

_____

_____

_____

_____

_____

_____

_____

My Personal History

My first child's full name at present: _____

☐   Child has never had any children born alive.

☐   Child has had _____ children born alive.

	Full Name of My Grandchild at Birth	Last Name at Present or at Death	Date of Birth	Death
Gch #1				
Gch #2				
Gch #3				
Gch #4				
Gch #5				
Gch #6				

	Name of Grandchild's Present Spouse	Address
Gch # 1		
Gch #2		
Gch #3		
Gch #4		
Gch #5		
Gch #6		

Gch - Grandchild

My Personal History

_____

_____

_____

_____

_____

_____

_____

_____

_____

_____

_____

_____

_____

_____

_____

_____

_____

_____

_____

_____

_____

_____

_____

_____

CHILDREN

My Personal History

Child's full name at present: _____
First   Middle   Last

Child's full name at birth: _____
First   Middle   Last

Date of birth: _____ Place of birth: _____

Adopted? _____ (If so, give details on reverse.)

Present address: _____
Street Address and Apartment Number

_____
City

_____
State   Zip Code

Date of death: _____ Cause of death: _____

Child is buried at _____
Name of Cemetery

_____
City   State

in Cemetery Lot #_____

Or: Child was cremated and the ashes were _____

_____

Or: Child donated body to _____
Name of Medical School

☐ Child has never married.

☐ Child has been married _____ times. The names of the child's spouses, marriage dates, etc., are as follows:

	Name of Spouse (before marriage)	Birth Date	Date of Marriage	Date of Death	Divorce
#1					
#2					
#3					

My Personal History

_____

_____

_____

_____

_____

_____

_____

_____

_____

_____

_____

_____

_____

_____

_____

_____

_____

_____

_____

_____

_____

_____

_____

_____

_____

My Personal History

My second child's full name at present: _____

☐   Child has never had any children born alive.

☐   Child has had _____ children born alive.

	Full Name of My Grandchild at Birth	Last Name at Present or at Death	Date of Birth	Death
Gch #1				
Gch #2				
Gch #3				
Gch #4				
Gch #5				
Gch #6				

	Name of Grandchild's Present Spouse	Address
Gch # 1		
Gch #2		
Gch #3		
Gch #4		
Gch #5		
Gch #6		

Gch - Grandchild

My Personal History

_____

_____

_____

_____

_____

_____

_____

_____

_____

_____

_____

_____

_____

_____

_____

_____

_____

_____

_____

_____

_____

_____

_____

_____

_____

_____

_____

My Personal History

Child's full name at present: _____

First   Middle   Last

Child's full name at birth: _____

First   Middle   Last

Date of birth: _____ Place of birth: _____

Adopted?_____ (If so, give details on reverse.)

Present address: _____

Street Address and Apartment Number

_____

City

_____

State   Zip Code

Date of death: _____ Cause of death: _____

Child is buried at _____

Name of Cemetery

_____

City   State

in Cemetery Lot #_____

Or: Child was cremated and the ashes were _____

_____

Or: Child donated body to _____

Name of Medical School

☐ Child has never married.

☐ Child has been married _____ times. The names of the child's spouses, marriage dates, etc., are as follows:

	Name of Spouse (at marriage)	Birth Date	Date of Marriage	Date of Death	Divorce
#1					
#2					
#3					

My Personal History

_____

_____

_____

_____

_____

_____

_____

_____

_____

_____

_____

_____

_____

_____

_____

_____

_____

_____

_____

_____

_____

_____

_____

_____

_____

My Personal History

My third child's full name at present: _____

☐ Child has never had any children born alive.

☐ Child has had _____ children born alive.

	Full Name of My Grandchild at Birth	Last Name at Present or at Death	Date of Birth	Death
Gch #1				
Gch #2				
Gch #3				
Gch #4				
Gch #5				
Gch #6				

	Name of Grandchild's Present Spouse	Address
Gch # 1		
Gch #2		
Gch #3		
Gch #4		
Gch #5		
Gch #6		

Gch - Grandchild

My Personal History

_____

_____

_____

_____

_____

_____

_____

_____

_____

_____

_____

_____

_____

_____

_____

_____

_____

_____

_____

_____

_____

_____

_____

_____

CHILDREN

My Personal History

Child's full name at present: _____

First   Middle   Last

Child's full name at birth: _____

First   Middle   Last

Date of birth: _____ Place of birth: _____

Adopted? _____ (If so, give details on reverse.)

Present address: _____

Street Address and Apartment Number

_____

City

_____

State   Zip Code

Date of death: _____ Cause of death: _____

Child is buried at _____

Name of Cemetery

_____

City   State

in Cemetery Lot # _____

Or: Child was cremated and the ashes were _____

_____

Or: Child donated body to _____

Name of Medical School

☐   Child has never married.

☐   Child has been married _____ times. The names of the child's spouses, marriage dates, etc., are
     as follows:

	Name of Spouse (before marriage)	Birth Date	Date of Marriage	Date of Death	Divorce
#1					
#2					
#3					

My Personal History

_____
_____
_____
_____
_____
_____
_____
_____
_____
_____
_____
_____
_____
_____
_____
_____
_____
_____
_____
_____
_____
_____
_____
_____
_____
_____

CHILDREN

My Personal History

My fourth child's full name at present: _____

☐ Child has never had any children born alive.

☐ Child has had _____ children born alive.

	Full Name of My Grandchild at Birth	Last Name at Present or at Death	Date of Birth	Death
Gch #1				
Gch #2				
Gch #3				
Gch #4				
Gch #5				
Gch #6				

	Name of Grandchild's Present Spouse	Address
Gch # 1		
Gch #2		
Gch #3		
Gch #4		
Gch #5		
Gch #6		

Gch - Grandchild

My Personal History

_____

_____

_____

_____

_____

_____

_____

_____

_____

_____

_____

_____

_____

_____

_____

_____

_____

_____

_____

_____

_____

_____

_____

My Personal History

Child's full name at present: _____

                                         First   *Middle*   *Last*

Child's full name at birth: _____

                                      First   *Middle*   *Last*

Date of birth: _____ Place of birth: _____

Adopted?_____ (If so, give details on reverse.)

Present address: _____

                          Street Address and Apartment Number

                          _____

                          City

                          _____

                          State   *Zip Code*

Date of death: _____ Cause of death: _____

Child is buried at _____

                    Name of Cemetery

                   _____

                   City   *State*

      in Cemetery Lot #_____

Or: Child was cremated and the ashes were _____

      _____

Or: Child donated body to _____

                          Name of Medical School

☐   Child has never married.

☐   Child has been married _____ times. The names of the child's spouses, marriage dates, etc., are as follows:

	Name of Spouse (before marriage)	Birth Date	Date of Marriage	Date of Death	Divorce
#1					
#2					
#3					

My Personal History

_____

_____

_____

_____

_____

_____

_____

_____

_____

_____

_____

_____

_____

_____

_____

_____

_____

_____

_____

_____

_____

_____

_____

_____

_____

My Personal History

My fifth child's full name at present: _____

☐   Child has never had any children born alive.

☐   Child has had _____ children born alive.

	Full Name of My Grandchild at Birth	Last Name at Present or at Death	Date of Birth	Death
Gch #1				
Gch #2				
Gch #3				
Gch #4				
Gch #5				
Gch #6				

	Name of Grandchild's Present Spouse	Address
Gch # 1		
Gch #2		
Gch #3		
Gch #4		
Gch #5		
Gch #6		

Gch - Grandchild

My Personal History

_____

_____

_____

_____

_____

_____

_____

_____

_____

_____

_____

_____

_____

_____

_____

_____

_____

_____

_____

_____

_____

_____

_____

_____

_____

My Personal History

Child's full name at present: _____

First   Middle   Last

Child's full name at birth: _____

First   Middle   Last

Date of birth: _____ Place of birth: _____

Adopted? _____ (If so, give details on reverse.)

Present address: _____

Street Address and Apartment Number

_____

City

_____

State   Zip Code

Date of death: _____ Cause of death: _____

Child is buried at _____

Name of Cemetery

_____

City   State

in Cemetery Lot #_____

Or: Child was cremated and the ashes were _____

_____

Or: Child donated body to _____

Name of Medical School

☐   Child has never married.

☐   Child has been married _____ times. The names of the child's spouses, marriage dates, etc., are as follows:

	Name of Spouse (before marriage)	Birth Date	Date of Marriage	Date of Death	Divorce
#1					
#2					
#3					

My Personal History

My Personal History

My sixth child's full name at present: _____

☐   Child has never had any children born alive.

☐   Child has had _____ children born alive.

	Full Name of My Grandchild at Birth	Last Name at Present or at Death	Date of Birth	Death
Gch #1				
Gch #2				
Gch #3				
Gch #4				
Gch #5				
Gch #6				

	Name of Grandchild's Present Spouse	Address
Gch # 1		
Gch #2		
Gch #3		
Gch #4		
Gch #5		
Gch #6		

Gch - Grandchild

My Personal History

_____

_____

_____

_____

_____

_____

_____

_____

_____

_____

_____

_____

_____

_____

_____

_____

_____

_____

_____

_____

_____

_____

_____

_____

FATHER

My Personal History

My father's full name at birth: _____
                  First   *Middle*   *Last*

Place of birth: _____
          City   *County*   *State*   *Country*

Date of birth: _____

Present address: _____
       Street Address and Apartment Number

_____
   City

_____
   State   *Zip Code*

Date of death: _____ Cause of death: _____

My father is buried at _____
        Name of Cemetery

_____
   City   *State*

      in Cemetery Lot # _____

Or: My father was cremated and his ashes were _____

_____

Or: My father donated his body to _____
                                    Name of Medical School

My parents were married on _____ at _____

_____
               City   *State*

My parents were divorced on _____ at _____
                          Date   *City*   *State*

My father was married _____ times.

	Name of Wife (before marriage)	Date of Marriage	Date of Death	Divorce
#1				
#2				
#3				

FATHER
My Personal History

_____

_____

_____

_____

_____

_____

_____

_____

_____

_____

_____

_____

_____

_____

_____

_____

_____

_____

_____

_____

_____

_____

_____

_____

_____

MOTHER

My Personal History

My mother's full name at present: _____
First   *First*   *Middle*   *Last*

My mother's full name at birth:_____
First   *Middle*   *Last*

Place of birth: _____
City   *County*   *State*   *Country*

Date of birth: _____

Present address: _____
Street Address and Apartment Number

_____
City

_____
State   *Zip Code*

Date of death: _____ Cause of death: _____

My mother is buried at _____
Name of Cemetery

_____
City   *State*

in Cemetery Lot #_____

Or: My mother was cremated and her ashes were_____

_____

Or: My mother donated her body to_____
Name of Medical School

My parents were married on _____ at _____

_____
City   *State*

My parents were divorced on_____ at _____
Date   *City*   *State*

My mother was married _____ times.

	Name of Husband	Date of Marriage	Date of Death	Date of Divorce
#1				
#2				
#3				

MOTHER

My Personal History

_____

_____

_____

_____

_____

_____

_____

_____

_____

_____

_____

_____

_____

_____

_____

_____

_____

_____

_____

_____

_____

_____

_____

_____

_____

_____

_____

My Personal History

GRANDFATHER

My grandfather's full name at birth: _____
First   Middle   Last

Place of birth: _____
City   County   State   Country

Date of birth: _____ Date of death: _____

Place of burial: _____
Cemetery   Lot No.

_____
City   State

My grandfather was married _____ times.

	Name of Wife (before marriage)	Date of Marriage	Date of Death	Divorce
#1				
#2				
#3				

GRANDMOTHER

My grandmother's full name at birth: _____
First   Middle   Last

Place of birth: _____
City   County   State   Country

Date of birth: _____ Date of death: _____

Place of burial: _____
Cemetery   Lot No.

_____
City   State

My grandmother was married _____ times.

	Name of Husband	Date of Marriage	Date of Death	Divorce
#1				
#2				
#3				

My Personal History

_____
_____
_____
_____
_____
_____
_____
_____
_____
_____
_____
_____
_____
_____
_____
_____
_____
_____
_____
_____
_____
_____
_____
_____
_____

GRANDPARENTS

My Personal History

GRANDFATHER

My grandfather's full name at birth: _____

        First   *Middle*   *Last*

Place of birth: _____

      City   *County*   *State*   *Country*

Date of birth: _____ Date of death: _____

Place of burial: _____

     Cemetery   *Lot No.*

_____

     City   *State*

My grandfather was married _____ times.

	Name of Wife (before marriage)	Date of Marriage	Date of Death	Divorce
#1				
#2				
#3				

GRANDMOTHER

My grandmother's full name at birth: _____

        First   *Middle*   *Last*

Place of birth: _____

      City   *County*   *State*   *Country*

Date of birth: _____ Date of death: _____

Place of burial: _____

     Cemetery   *Lot No.*

_____

     City   *State*

My grandmother was married _____ times.

	Name of Husband	Date of Marriage	Date of Death	Divorce
#1				
#2				
#3				

My Personal History

_____

_____

_____

_____

_____

_____

_____

_____

_____

_____

_____

_____

_____

_____

_____

_____

_____

_____

_____

_____

_____

_____

_____

_____

_____

_____

_____

_____

_____

My Personal History

Full name at present: _____

                          First   *Middle*   *Last*

Full name at birth: _____

                          First   *Middle*   *Last*

Place of birth: _____

            City   *County*   *State*   *Country*

Date of birth: _____ Date of death: _____

This sibling is related to me by: ☐ full blood   ☐ half blood   ☐ adoption
                                         (common parents)   (one common parent)

If related by half blood, or adopted, sibling's parents (or adopting parents) were:

Mother: _____

Father: _____

Sibling's present address: _____

                               Street Address and Apartment Number

_____

Tel. #   *City*   *State*   *Zip Code*

Sibling is buried at: _____

                 Cemetery   *Lot No.*

_____

                 City   *State*

☐ Sibling has never married.   ☐ Sibling has been married _____ times.

	Name of Spouse (before marriage)	Date of Marriage	Date of Death	Divorce
#1				
#2				
#3				

☐ Sibling has had _____ children born alive, or adopted; or, ☐ sibling has never had any children.

	Full Name of Child at Birth (My nieces and nephews)	Last Name at Present or at Death	Date of Birth	Death
#1				
#2				
#3				
#4				
#5				
#6				

My Personal History

_____
_____
_____
_____
_____
_____
_____
_____
_____
_____
_____
_____
_____
_____
_____
_____
_____
_____
_____
_____
_____
_____
_____
_____
_____
_____

My Personal History

Full name at present: _____

                                        First   *Middle*   *Last*

Full name at birth: _____

                                First   *Middle*   *Last*

Place of birth: _____

                  City   *County*   *State*   *Country*

Date of birth: _____ Date of death: _____

This sibling is related to me by: □ full blood   □ half blood   □ adoption
                                    (common parents)   (one common parent)

If related by half blood, or adopted, sibling's parents (or adopting parents) were:

  Mother: _____

  Father: _____

Sibling's present address: _____

                           Street Address and Apartment Number

_____

Tel. #   *City*   *State*   *Zip Code*

Sibling is buried at: _____

                 Cemetery   *Lot No.*

_____

                 City   *State*

□ Sibling has never married.   □ Sibling has been married _____ times.

	Name of Spouse (before marriage)	Date of Marriage	Date of Death	Divorce
#1				
#2				
#3				

□ Sibling has had _____ children born alive, or adopted; or, □ sibling has never had any children.

	Full Name of Child at Birth (My nieces and nephews)	Last Name at Present or at Death	Date of Birth	Death
#1				
#2				
#3				
#4				
#5				
#6				

My Personal History

_____

_____

_____

_____

_____

_____

_____

_____

_____

_____

_____

_____

_____

_____

_____

_____

_____

_____

_____

_____

_____

_____

My Personal History

Full name at present: _____
First   Middle   Last

Full name at birth: _____
First   Middle   Last

Place of birth: _____
City   County   State   Country

Date of birth: _____ Date of death: _____

This sibling is related to me by: □ full blood   □ half blood   □ adoption
(common parents)   (one common parent)

If related by half blood, or adopted, sibling's parents (or adopting parents) were:

Mother: _____

Father: _____

Sibling's present address: _____
Street Address and Apartment Number

_____
Tel. #   City   State   Zip Code

Sibling is buried at: _____
Cemetery   Lot No.

_____
City   State

□ Sibling has never married.   □ Sibling has been married _____ times.

	Name of Spouse (before marriage)	Date of Marriage	Date of Death	Divorce
#1				
#2				
#3				

□ Sibling has had _____ children born alive, or adopted; or, □ sibling has never had any children.

	Full Name of Child at Birth (My nieces and nephews)	Last Name at Present or at Death	Date of Birth	Death
#1				
#2				
#3				
#4				
#5				
#6				

My Personal History

_____

_____

_____

_____

_____

_____

_____

_____

_____

_____

_____

_____

_____

_____

_____

_____

_____

_____

_____

_____

_____

_____

_____

My Personal History

Full name at present: _____
                                      First   *Middle*   *Last*

Full name at birth: _____
                              First   *Middle*   *Last*

Place of birth: _____
                City   *County*   *State*   *Country*

Date of birth: _____ Date of death: _____

This sibling is related to me by: □ full blood   □ half blood   □ adoption
                                          (common parents)   (one common parent)

If related by half blood, or adopted, sibling's parents (or adopting parents) were:

  Mother: _____

  Father: _____

Sibling's present address: _____
                                  Street Address and Apartment Number

_____ _____
Tel. #   *City*   *State*   *Zip Code*

Sibling is buried at: _____
                  Cemetery   *Lot No.*

_____
              City   *State*

□ Sibling has never married.   □ Sibling has been married _____ times.

	Name of Spouse (before marriage)	Date of Marriage	Date of Death	Divorce
#1				
#2				
#3				

□ Sibling has had _____ children born alive, or adopted; or, □ sibling has never had any children.

	Full Name of Child at Birth (My nieces and nephews)	Last Name at Present or at Death	Date of Birth	Death
#1				
#2				
#3				
#4				
#5				
#6				

My Personal History

_____

_____

_____

_____

_____

_____

_____

_____

_____

_____

_____

_____

_____

_____

_____

_____

_____

_____

_____

_____

_____

_____

_____

_____

_____

_____

_____

_____

My Personal History

Full name at present: _____
First   Middle   Last

Full name at birth: _____
First   Middle   Last

Place of birth: _____
City   County   State   Country

Date of birth: _____ Date of death: _____

This sibling is related to me by: □ full blood   □ half blood   □ adoption
(common parents)   (one common parent)

If related by half blood, or adopted, sibling's parents (or adopting parents) were:

Mother: _____

Father: _____

Sibling's present address: _____
Street Address and Apartment Number

_____
Tel. #   City   State   Zip Code

Sibling is buried at: _____
Cemetery   Lot No.

_____
City   State

□ Sibling has never married.   □ Sibling has been married _____ times.

	Name of Spouse (before marriage)	Date of Marriage	Date of Death	Divorce
#1				
#2				
#3				

□ Sibling has had _____ children born alive, or adopted; or, □ sibling has never had any children.

	Full Name of Child at Birth (My nieces and nephews)	Last Name at Present or at Death	Date of Birth	Death
#1				
#2				
#3				
#4				
#5				
#6				

My Personal History

_____

_____

_____

_____

_____

_____

_____

_____

_____

_____

_____

_____

_____

_____

_____

_____

_____

_____

_____

_____

_____

_____

_____

_____

_____

_____

EDUCATIONAL BACKGROUND

My Personal History

I attended the following elementary schools:

Name of School	Location	Grades Attended	Dates Attended

I attended the following junior high schools (or middle schools):

Name of School	Location	Grades Attended	Dates Attended

I attended the following high schools (or preparatory schools):

Name of School	Location	Grades Attended	Dates Attended

I □ did not graduate, or □ graduated from the last-named school in _____ .

I attended the following institutions of higher learning:

Name of Institution	Location	Degree	Dates Attended

EDUCATIONAL BACKGROUND

My Personal History

I was involved in the following extra-curricular activities: (List athletics, debating, drama, music, art, journalism, etc.)

_____

_____

_____

_____

_____

_____

_____

_____

_____

I received the following educational honors, scholarships, commendations, etc.: (List details.)

_____

_____

_____

_____

_____

_____

_____

_____

WORK BACKGROUND

My Personal History

The following is a list of my primary employers:

Names of Primary Employers	Location	Dates	Type of Work

☐   I retired from work _____ .

☐   I am presently employed: (describe name and address of employer, or place of self-employment, the type of work, etc.)

_____

_____

_____

_____

_____

Describe any interesting facts, over the years, concerning employment:

_____

_____

_____

_____

(may be continued on reverse)

WORK BACKGROUND

My Personal History

_____

_____

_____

_____

_____

_____

_____

_____

_____

_____

_____

_____

_____

_____

_____

_____

_____

_____

_____

_____

_____

_____

_____

_____

RELIGION, POLITICS & HOBBIES

My Personal History

My religious memberships, activities and beliefs are as follows:

_____

_____

_____

_____

_____

_____

My political memberships, activities and beliefs are as follows:

_____

_____

_____

_____

_____

_____

Over the years, my hobbies have been:

_____

_____

_____

_____

_____

(Any of the above may be continued on the reverse side of this page)

_____

RELIGION, POLITICS & HOBBIES

My Personal History

_____

_____

_____

_____

_____

_____

_____

_____

_____

_____

_____

_____

_____

_____

_____

_____

_____

_____

_____

_____

_____

_____

_____

_____

ORGANIZATIONS, UNIONS, CLUBS, ETC.

My Personal History

I have belonged to the following organizations, unions, clubs, etc. (List all such organizations, with dates of membership, offices held, etc. If the organization is not commonly know, describe it.)

_____

_____

_____

_____

_____

_____

_____

_____

_____

_____

_____

_____

_____

_____

_____

_____

_____

_____

_____

PLACES OF RESIDENCE

My Personal History

I have lived in the following towns, cities and states at the street addresses listed:

Address	City	State	Dates

MISCELLANEOUS

My Personal History

The following miscellaneous notes regarding my personal history may be of interest to my heirs:

_____

_____

_____

_____

_____

_____

_____

_____

_____

_____

_____

_____

_____

_____

_____

_____

_____

_____

_____

MISCELLANEOUS

My Personal History

_____

_____

_____

_____

_____

_____

_____

_____

_____

_____

_____

_____

_____

_____

_____

_____

_____

_____

_____

_____

_____

_____

_____

_____

_____

Insurance offers a way to spread the risk of financial loss among many people. The payment of an annual premium protects the insured (to the limits of the policy) against losses from fire, theft, accident, liability, etc. Any loss is shared by all of those insured, saving the individual from financial disaster. The group, in other words, absorbs the unexpected losses of the individual.

Life insurance is primarily intended to ease the financial loss to a beneficiary that results from the policyholder's death. Although death comes to everyone and cannot be considered "unexpected" in the long run, it can certainly be unexpected when it occurs. If something should happen to you — death, an accident, a stroke, or other circumstance which prevents you from acting on your own behalf — your loved ones may have to file claims, cancel certain policies or obtain new ones in order to protect your property. There are also many policies that go unclaimed because the family or heirs were never told about them. For these reasons, it is important that your loved ones know about all of your insurance policies. The forms in this chapter are provided to list your various policies with the names and addresses of the agents and companies.

The following is not a detailed breakdown of the many types of insurance available. It should, however, give you some information about the most widely used coverages in order to help you organize your own policies.

LIFE INSURANCE

A life insurance policy pays a designated sum of money to the beneficiary upon the death of the insured. This money may be paid in a lump sum, in a monthly sum for the life of another, in monthly sums over a certain period of time, or in some other manner spelled out by the terms of the policy. Regardless of the method of payment, the sum is designated in the provisions of the policy.

A widely purchased form of life insurance is *whole life insurance.* This type of coverage provides a sum of money (face value) to be paid to the beneficiary at the time of the insured's death. The insured has paid the same annual premium since taking out the policy. The amount of the premium is determined by the age of the individual at the time the policy was purchased. The younger the purchaser, the smaller the premium on the policy. Variations in the method of payment for whole life insurance are available. For example, you might obtain a policy which requires annual premiums for 20 years. At the expiration of the 20-year period, the policy continues in effect for the balance of your life, but no more premiums are required. It is even possible to purchase a policy by making one large initial premium payment. Regardless of the method of payment, whole life insurance provides coverage for the rest of your life.

Term insurance, on the other hand, provides insurance coverage only for a specified length of time. That is, you might purchase a policy which provides coverage for 5-years, 10-years or 20-years. The annual premium for term insurance is substantially less than the annual premium for whole life insurance. For example, a typical annual premium for a five-year term policy might be $3-$4 per $1,000 at age 25. The cost of purchasing the same coverage would gradually increase with the age of the purchaser. By age 55, that same coverage could run between $15 and $20 per $1,000, or about five times the price given a 25-year-old. On the other hand, whole life insurance might start around $10 per $1,000 at age 25. The premiums would remain at that level throughout the life of the insured. To take out the same coverage at age 55, however, might run from $40 to $70 per $1,000, or four to seven times the price given a 25-year-old.

Many term life insurance contracts provide that the policy may be renewed at the end of the term without providing further proof of insurability. The premium for the renewed term will be higher than for the original term. Other term policies provide that they may be converted, within a certain period of time, into whole life or endowment insurance without proof of insurability. Once again, the premium would be adjusted.

With *endowment insurance*, the insurance company agrees to pay the face value to the beneficiary if the insured dies during a specified number of years, and to the insured if he outlives the specified number of years. For example, a $20,000 20-year endowment policy will pay the insured $20,000 if he is living at the end of 20 years but will pay $20,000 to the beneficiary if the insured dies within the 20-year period. The endowment policy has the most expensive premium. For a person 25 years of age buying a 20-year endowment policy, the premiums would be about $40 a year per $1,000 of insurance.

❖❖❖❖❖

Regardless of the type of life insurance held by the insured, it is important that the insurance policies be readily available at death, that the heirs know their location, and that they be kept in a safe place. The policy must be surrendered to the insuring company at the time of payment of the proceeds. Although there is a procedure which may be followed in the case of a lost policy, there may be a long delay in collecting the proceeds from the company.

Many employers provide life insurance for employees. Partnerships often fund buy-sell agreements with life insurance. Be sure to include information about work-related insurance in the forms.

MEDICAL, HEALTH, DISABILITY, ACCIDENT AND TRAVEL INSURANCE

Health insurance provides a means for paying hospital and medical expenses arising from sickness and accident. In addition, disability insurance policies are available to provide money for loss of income when an individual is unable to work because of sickness or accidental injury.

There are many different types of accident and illness insurance policies. Some are so limited in scope that it seems necessary "to be gored by a bull while riding a streetcar between the hours of midnight and 3:00 a.m." in order to collect on the policy. Other policies, however, provide very broad coverage, though each has its limitations.

Travel policies were the forerunners of the present-day health and accident policies. Travel policies may limit coverage to airplanes, automobiles, boats and motorcycles; or, they may cover an insured individual during a specified policy period, like the length of a vacation or business trip.

Medical expense reimbursement policies range from a policy which pays $10 for each day the insured is hospitalized, to policies which cover almost every health expense which could be incurred by the policyholder. Because the coverages vary to such a great extent, there is a wide range in the cost of health and accident coverage.

During the last three or four decades, Blue Cross-Blue Shield plans have been widely used throughout the country. A relatively new idea in health care insurance that is gaining popularity is offered through Health Maintenance Organization plans (HMO's). This form of health insurance enables a person to contract with a group of physicians who have joined together to provide specific health services for a designated annual fee. The HMO group may offer its services in a certain hospital or clinic, or the physicians within the group may be scattered in offices and hospitals throughout the community. (The latter is known as an Independent Practice Association, or IPA.) In addition, *major medical coverage* is available to pick up expenses not covered by a basic health and accident policy.

AUTOMOBILE INSURANCE

Automobile insurance should be considered a necessity by the owner of any motor vehicle. In fact, many states require all drivers to be insured for liability to other persons for damages resulting from an automobile accident. Regardless of the law, it only makes good sense to insure yourself against the claims of others and against a loss that you might sustain as the result of collision, fire or theft of your automobile.

Liability coverage protects you, to the extent of the coverage that you have purchased, against the claims of persons who claim to have been injured or damaged as a result of the operation of your motor vehicle. The policy not only provides for payment of the claim, but pays legal and other expenses for the defense of any claim.

Collision coverage pays for damage sustained by your automobile in a collision or upset. It is usually subject to a deductible amount which you must pay.

Comprehensive coverage, along with fire, theft and windstorm coverage, protects the insured from damage (other than damage caused by accident) to his own automobile.

Uninsured motorists' insurance protects the persons in the insured vehicle when involved in an accident with an uninsured motorist. The insurance, for all practical purposes, provides liability coverage for the uninsured motorist; and the injured persons can look to their own insurance company to cover their losses — rather than to an uncollectible individual.

Underinsured motorists' insurance protects the person in the insured vehicle involved in an accident with a motorist who is underinsured. If, for example, the person in the insured vehicle sustained $50,000 of personal injuries because of the negligence of a motorist who only has $20,000 of liability coverage, the underinsured motorists' insurance would pay the excess over $20,000 up to the coverage limits purchased by the insured.

No-fault liability for motor vehicle accidents has been adopted by about half of the states. Although there are wide variations in the provisions of the different laws, the general idea of no-fault liability is that the automobile owner must provide his own insurance for any injuries or property damage he sustains regardless of who was to blame for the accident.

Except in certain circumstances (as established by the State's no-fault law), he cannot sue the other driver to recover any damages. In those States which have adopted the no-fault concept, the law requires that motorists maintain no-fault insurance on their vehicles. Generally, if you do not carry no-fault insurance, you are not only violating the law, but you have no place to seek repayment of your losses, even if you are not at fault in an accident.

TO YOUR HEIRS:

At time of death, the automobile insurance company should be notified so there will be complete coverage during the time period before its assignment to its next owner.

RESIDENCE INSURANCE

Originally, fire insurance was about the only type of insurance that a home owner could obtain on his residence. As the various insurance lines developed, insurance became available to protect against windstorm, hail, explosion, riot, smoke damage, etc. Insurance also became available for the contents of the home, as well as for outbuildings.

Today, most homeowners purchase a "homeowners policy" which combines fire and extended coverage insurance on the dwelling with protection for personal property, additional living expense, comprehensive personal liability coverage, medical payments, and physical damage to property of others. Rather than being required to search out individual policies covering all of these various risks, the homeowners policy combines them in one.

Similar types of policies are available to the condominium owner and apartment dweller. The policy can be tailor-made to fit specific needs by the addition of standard forms.

Upon your death, your heirs should immediately contact your insurance agent to assure that your home and contents are properly insured during the administration of your estate.

LIFE INSURANCE

My Insurance

Types of Insurance: *WH – Whole Life*   *TM – Term*   *EN – Endowment*   *DI – Double Indemnity*
O – Other

Company: _____

Agent (if any): _____

Address of ☐ Company, or, ☐ Agent: _____

_____

_____

Policy #: _____ Face amount: _____ Type: _____

Beneficiary(ies): _____

❖❖❖❖❖❖

Company: _____

Agent (if any): _____

Address of ☐ Company, or, ☐ Agent: _____

_____

_____

Policy #: _____ Face amount: _____ Type: _____

Beneficiary(ies): _____

❖❖❖❖❖❖

Company: _____

Agent (if any): _____

Address of ☐ Company, or ☐ Agent: _____

_____

_____

Policy #: _____ Face amount: _____ Type: _____

Beneficiary(ies): _____

LIFE INSURANCE

My Insurance

Types of Insurance: *WH — Whole Life*   *TM — Term*   *EN — Endowment*   *DI — Double Indemnity*
O — Other

Company: _____

Agent (if any): _____

Address of □ Company, or, □ Agent: _____

_____

_____

Policy #: _____ Face amount: _____ Type: _____

Beneficiary(ies): _____

❖❖❖❖❖❖

Company: _____

Agent (if any): _____

Address of □ Company, or, □ Agent: _____

_____

_____

Policy #: _____ Face amount: _____ Type: _____

Beneficiary(ies): _____

❖❖❖❖❖❖

Company: _____

Agent (if any): _____

Address of □ Company, or □ Agent: _____

_____

_____

Policy #: _____ Face amount: _____ Type: _____

Beneficiary(ies): _____

LIFE INSURANCE

My Insurance

Types of Insurance: *WH — Whole Life*   *TM — Term*   *EN — Endowment*   *DI — Double Indemnity*
O — Other

Company: _____

Agent (if any): _____

Address of ☐ Company, or, ☐ Agent: _____

_____

_____

Policy #: _____ Face amount: _____ Type: _____

Beneficiary(ies): _____

❖❖❖❖❖❖

Company: _____

Agent (if any): _____

Address of ☐ Company, or, ☐ Agent: _____

_____

_____

Policy #: _____ Face amount: _____ Type: _____

Beneficiary(ies): _____

❖❖❖❖❖❖

Company: _____

Agent (if any): _____

Address of ☐ Company, or ☐ Agent: _____

_____

_____

Policy #: _____ Face amount: _____ Type: _____

Beneficiary(ies): _____

RESIDENCE INSURANCE

My Insurance

I carry residence insurance with the following companies: (List all policies including fire, windstorm, theft, personal liability, homeowners, etc.)

Company: _____ Policy # _____

Agent (if any): _____

Address of ☐ Company, or ☐ Agent: _____

_____

_____

Description of coverage: _____

_____

❖❖❖❖❖❖

Company: _____ Policy # _____

Agent (if any): _____

Address of ☐ Company, or ☐ Agent: _____

_____

_____

Description of coverage: _____

_____

❖❖❖❖❖❖

Company: _____ Policy # _____

Agent (if any): _____

Address of ☐ Company, or ☐ Agent: _____

_____

_____

Description of coverage: _____

_____

MEDICAL INSURANCE, ETC.

My Insurance

Types of Insurance:

HO – *Hospitalization*   SU – *Surgical*   MD – *Medical*
MM – *Major Medical*   TR – *Travel Accidental*   ATR – *Air Travel*
DI – *Disability*   *Death*   *Accidental Death*
                             O – *Other*   MC – *Medicare*

Company: _____

Agent (if any): _____

Address of ☐ Company, or, ☐ Agent: _____

_____

_____

Policy #, Group #, Service Code #, etc.: _____

_____ Type of Policy (HO, MD, etc.): _____

❖❖❖❖❖❖

Company: _____

Agent (if any): _____

Address of ☐ Company, or, ☐ Agent: _____

_____

_____

Policy #, Group #, Service Code #, etc.: _____

_____ Type of Policy (HO, MD, etc.): _____

❖❖❖❖❖❖

Company: _____

Agent (if any): _____

Address of ☐ Company, or ☐ Agent: _____

_____

_____

Policy #, Group #, Service Code #, etc.: _____

_____ Type of Policy (HO, MD, etc.): _____

MEDICAL INSURANCE, ETC.

Medical, Health,
Disability, Accident & Travel

My Insurance

Types of Insurance:

HO – Hospitalization   SU – Surgical   MD – Medical
MM – Major Medical   TR – Travel Accidental   ATR – Air Travel
DI – Disability   Death   Accidental Death
       O – Other   MC – Medicare

Company: _____

Agent (if any): _____

Address of ☐ Company, or, ☐ Agent: _____

Policy #, Group #, Service Code #, etc.: _____

Type of Policy (HO, MD, etc.): _____

❖❖❖❖❖

Company: _____

Agent (if any): _____

Address of ☐ Company, or, ☐ Agent: _____

Policy #, Group #, Service Code #, etc.: _____

Type of Policy (HO, MD, etc.): _____

❖❖❖❖❖

Company: _____

Agent (if any): _____

Address of ☐ Company, or ☐ Agent: _____

Policy #, Group #, Service Code #, etc.: _____

Type of Policy (HO, MD, etc.): _____

VEHICLE INSURANCE

Automobiles,
Motorcycles, Boats, Planes, etc.

My Insurance

I carry automobile insurance (including motorcycles, snowmobiles, boats, airplanes, etc.) with the following companies:

Company: _____ Policy # _____

Agent (if any): _____

Address of ☐ Company, or ☐ Agent: _____

_____

_____

Description of vehicles insured: _____

_____

❖❖❖❖❖❖

Company: _____ Policy # _____

Agent (if any): _____

Address of ☐ Company, or ☐ Agent: _____

_____

_____

Description of vehicles insured: _____

_____

❖❖❖❖❖❖

Company: _____ Policy # _____

Agent (if any): _____

Address of ☐ Company, or ☐ Agent: _____

_____

_____

Description of vehicles insured: _____

_____

My Insurance

I carry automobile insurance (including motorcycles, snowmobiles, boats, airplanes, etc.) with the following companies:

Company: _____ Policy #_____

Agent (if any): _____

Address of ☐ Company, or ☐ Agent: _____

_____

_____

Description of vehicles insured: _____

_____

❖❖❖❖❖❖

Company: _____ Policy #_____

Agent (if any): _____

Address of ☐ Company, or ☐ Agent: _____

_____

_____

Description of vehicles insured: _____

_____

❖❖❖❖❖❖

Company: _____ Policy #_____

Agent (if any): _____

Address of ☐ Company, or ☐ Agent: _____

_____

_____

Description of vehicles insured: _____

_____

Most of us are aware of retirement benefits from Social Security, certain disability benefits for U.S. military veterans, Worker's Disability Compensation for job-related injuries and illness, and retirement payments from private and public pension plans. But some may be unaware of the benefits from the same sources which may be available to their survivors. This chapter is primarily concerned with benefits which may be available to your survivors.

SOCIAL SECURITY

Social Security provides continuing income when family earnings are reduced or stopped because of retirement, disability or death. Nine of ten workers in the United States earn protection under Social Security. The country's aged population has health insurance under Medicare.

Since Social Security legislation was enacted in 1935, there have been many changes to broaden the protection given to workers and their families. Initially, Social Security covered only the worker upon his retirement; but in 1939 the law was extended to pay certain dependents when he retired, as well as paying his survivors when he died.

Disability insurance benefits were first provided in July, 1957, giving workers protection against loss of earnings due to total disability.

The Social Security program was expanded again in 1965 with the enactment of Medicare which assured hospital and medical insurance protection to people 65 and over. Since 1973, Medicare coverage has been available to those people under 65 who have been entitled to Social Security disability checks for two or more consecutive years. It also covers people with permanent kidney failure who need dialysis or kidney transplants.

Before you or your family can receive monthly cash benefits, credit must be established for a certain amount of work under Social Security. The required work credit depends on your age and whether you are applying for retirement, survivor or disability benefits. Information on specific requirements is available at any of the 1300 Social Security Administration offices located throughout the country.

Retirement checks may be received as early as age 62 and disability checks at any age. Monthly payments can be received by a *retired* or *disabled* worker's:

- unmarried children under 18 (or 19 if full-time high school student);
- unmarried children 18 or over who were severely disabled before age 22, and who continue to be disabled;
- a wife or husband 62 or older; or,
- a wife under 62 if she cares for a child (under 16 or disabled) of the worker who is entitled to benefits based on the worker's earnings.

Your heirs are primarily affected, however, by benefits which may be available after your death. First, there is a lump-sum payment which can be made where an eligible husband or wife survive or there is a child entitled to survivor benefits.

Monthly payments can be made to a *deceased* worker's:

- unmarried children under 18 (or 19 if full-time high school student);
- unmarried son or daughter 18 or over who was severely disabled before 22 and who continues to be disabled;
- widow or widower 60 or older;
- widow or widower, or surviving divorced mother if caring for the worker's child (under 16 or disabled) who is getting a benefit based on the earnings of the deceased worker;
- widow or widower (50 or older) who becomes disabled not later than seven years after worker's death;
- dependent parents 62 or older; or,
- a surviving divorced spouse (62 or older) or a disabled surviving divorced spouse (50 or older), if the marriage lasted 10 or more years (20 years before January, 1979).

A marriage must have lasted at least one year before monthly benefits are available to the spouse of a *retired* or *disabled* worker; but the surviving spouse of a *deceased* worker can get benefits in most cases if the marriage lasted only nine months.

Medicare, a federal hospital and medical insurance, is available through Social Security to help protect people 65 and over from the high costs of health care. Also eligible for Medicare are disabled people under 65 who have been entitled to Social Security disability benefits for 24 or more consecutive months. Insured workers and their dependents who need dialysis treatment or a kidney transplant because of permanent kidney failure also have Medicare protection.

The *hospital insurance* portion of Medicare helps pay the cost of inpatient hospital care and certain kinds of follow-up care. If you are eligible for Social Security or Railroad Retirement payments, either as a worker, dependent, or survivor, you automatically have *hospital* insurance protection when you are 65.

The *medical insurance* portion of Medicare helps defray costs of physicians' services, outpatient hospital services, and certain other medical items, as well as services not covered by the hospital insurance. People who have medical insurance pay a monthly premium, but more than two-thirds of the cost of the medical insurance is paid from general revenues of the federal government. Only a small basic premium is charged for the medical insurance. The amount of the premium is adjusted periodically to reflect the cost of the care.

You should apply for your Medicare insurance at least three months before your 65th birthday in order that your protection will start at age 65.

APPLYING FOR SOCIAL SECURITY BENEFITS

When you apply for Social Security benefits, you should have with you:

- your own Social Security card or a record of your number (if your claim is on another person's record, you will need that person's card or a record of the number);

- proof of your age (a birth certificate or baptismal certificate made at or shortly after birth);
- your marriage certificate if you are applying for wife's or widow's benefits;
- your children's birth certificates if you are applying for them; and,
- your W-2 Form(s) for the previous year or a copy of your last federal income tax return if you are self-employed. Without this information, those earnings will not be in the Social Security records and cannot be included when your benefits are calculated.

❖❖❖❖❖

The above information will provide you and your heirs knowledge of certain rights which may be available to you or to them. *Since the Social Security Act can be amended at any time, this may not be the latest available information concerning benefits to which you or your heirs may be entitled. Contact the nearest Social Security Administration office for a full explanation of your rights under the law.*

VETERAN BENEFITS

The Veteran's Administration is charged with administering benefits available to persons who have served on active duty in the U.S. military service. The benefits depend upon the veteran's length of service, the era during which the service was performed, whether or not he is disabled, whether the disability was caused by active service, and so many other criteria that it would take another book to set out the specific requirements.

Under certain circumstances, the following benefits (and many more) *may* be available to a veteran:

- pensions for disability caused by service-connected injury or disease;
- pensions for certain non-service-connected disabilities;
- automobile allowance for service-connected loss, or permanent loss of the use of one or both hands or feet;
- hospitalization benefits;
- alcohol and drug dependence treatment;
- outpatient medical treatment;
- prosthetic appliances;
- vocational rehabilitation;
- loan guaranty benefits;
- insurance;
- federal civil service preference.

Certain benefits are available to your heirs if you were separated from the service under conditions other than dishonorable.

Burial flag. An American flag may be issued to drape the casket of an eligible veteran. After the funeral service, the flag may be given to the next of kin or close friend or associate of the deceased. Flags are issued at any VA office and most local post offices.

Burial in National Cemeteries. Any deceased veteran of wartime or peacetime service whose last period of active service terminated other than dishonorably may be buried in a National Cemetery. In addition, the spouse, surviving spouse or minor children of an eligible veteran may be buried in a National Cemetery. In each instance, space must be available. There is no charge for a grave nor for its opening and closing.

Transportation of deceased veteran to a National Cemetery. The VA may pay the cost of transportation of a deceased veteran for burial in a National Cemetery if the veteran died of a service-connected disability or the veteran was receiving disability compensation from the VA.

Headstones or markers. The VA will furnish, upon request, a headstone or marker to be placed at the unmarked grave of a veteran whose last discharge was other than dishonorable. This service is provided for eligible veterans whether they are buried in a National Cemetery or elsewhere. A headstone or marker is automatically furnished if burial is in a National Cemetery. Otherwise, application must be made to the VA. They will ship the headstone or marker, without charge, to the person or firm designated on the application. If a non-government headstone or marker is used at a veteran's gravesite in other than a National Cemetery, a partial reimbursement may be made by the VA. The amount of this payment would not exceed the average actual cost of a government headstone or marker.

Reimbursement of burial expenses. The VA is authorized to pay an allowance toward the funeral and burial expenses of an eligible veteran. A veteran not buried in a National Cemetery will be paid an additional allowance for a plot for interment. If the veteran's death is service-connected, the VA is authorized to pay a larger sum for the burial and funeral expenses.

Dependency and Indemnity Compensation (DIC). DIC payments are authorized for widows or widowers, children and parents of service personnel who die during active duty as well as veterans whose deaths were service-connected (when death occured on or after January 1, 1957). The exact amount of the basic benefit is determined by the military pay grade of the deceased veteran. Payments are also made for children between 18 and 23 attending school.

Non-service-connected death pension. Surviving spouses and unmarried children under age 18 (or until age 23 if attending an approved course of study) may be eligible for a pension if their income does not exceed certain limits.

Education for spouses, widows, widowers, sons and daughters. If a veteran is completely disabled or dies as a result of service, the VA will generally (but with some exceptions) pay to help educate the spouse, widow or widower, and each son and daughter beyond the secondary school level.

If you are a veteran, your heirs should seek assistance through the Veteran's Administration, or through a local Veteran's Counseling Service, in order to apply for available benefits.

WORKER'S COMPENSATION

Worker's compensation laws have been adopted by all of the States. Although details vary greatly, the general purpose is to provide income to workers who are unable to work as a result of an injury, or occupational disease, arising out of the worker's employment. While incapacitated, he received a weekly sum based upon his average wage and the number of his dependents. In addition, medical expenses related to the injury are paid by the employer or the employer's insurance company.

Here, however, we are primarily interested in worker's compensation benefits available to dependents of a deceased employee. Ordinarily, the spouse and minor children of an employee who died as the result of a work-incurred accident, or occupational disease, are entitled to weekly payments for a period of time. Usually, the wife is entitled to payments for a specified number of years or until her remarriage, whichever is sooner; and the dependent children are entitled to benefits until they reach a certain age.

Usually, the laws also provide that the widowed spouse, or the deceased employee's estate, is entitled to a specific funeral or death benefit.

It is important, then, that your heirs be made aware of any life-threatening injuries or occupational diseases incurred during the course of your employment. If your death is subsequently caused by the injury or occupational disease, your dependents may be entitled to substantial monetary benefits.

In the forms provided at the end of this chapter, be sure to detail any of your medical problems which may be related to your employment.

PENSIONS

Many public and private employees are provided pensions through their jobs. Some pensions are entirely financed by the employer, while some are co-financed by the employer and the employee.

Many persons not covered by a pension through their employment have established *Individual Retirement Accounts (IRA's)*. An IRA allows a person to deposit a certain sum of money annually in interest-bearing accounts while deferring taxation on the interest it earns until it is withdrawn at retirement.
retirement.

From the standpoint of your heirs, it is most vital that they be aware of any plans in which you are a member. At your death, the particular plan may provide dependency payments to your spouse and/or minor children; may provide a substantial pay-off to a designated beneficiary or to your estate; or may, in fact, provide nothing.

Self-employed individuals may establish a *Keogh pension plan*. This allows for larger, tax-free yearly investments and greater benefits than does the IRA.

In the forms provided at the end of the chapter, give all of the information to your heirs about any pension plans in which you have an interest.

SOCIAL SECURITY

My Other Benefits

My name (from Soc. Sec. card): _____

Soc. Sec. #:_____ □ Male, or, □ Female.

I □ have; or, □ have never filed an application for monthly Social Security benefits.

If so, said application was filed on □ my earning record; or, □ the earning record of:

_____

            Full name   *Social Security Number*

I received the following kind of monthly benefit:_____
                                            (retirement, disability, widow, etc.)

I □ have worked; or, □ have not worked in the railroad industry at any time after January 1, 1937.*

My military service information is found on my "Veteran's Benefits" form.

My marriage history and the facts related to my children are found in the forms located at the end of Chapter 1.

My Medicare information is found in the forms on pages 73-74.

My Social Security card is located:_____

Other documents pertaining to my Social Security status are located: _____

_____

This may affect your Social Security.

VETERAN'S BENEFITS

My Other Benefits

☐   I have never served in the military service of the United States.

☐   I have served in the military service of the United States.

Full present name: _____
                      First   *Middle*   *Last*

Name served under: _____
                      First   *Middle*   *Last*

V.A. File #: C-_____ Soc. Sec. #: _____ R.R. Ret. #: _____

Date of birth: _____ Place of birth: _____

Entered Active Service		Service Number	Separated		Grade or Rank and Branch
Date	Place		Date	Place	

My marriage history and the facts related to my children and my parents are found in the forms at the end of Chapter 1.

My military separation papers are located: _____

_____

I received the following military decorations: _____

_____

The following is a resume of my military career: _____

_____

_____

_____

_____

(may be continued on reverse)

VETERAN'S BENEFITS

My Other Benefits

WORKMEN'S COMPENSATION

My Other Benefits

☐ I have never received Workmen's Compensation benefits.

☐ I have received Workmen's Compensation benefits.

Name of employer: _____

Address of employer: _____

_____

_____

Date of injury or occupational disease: _____

Name of insurance company: _____

Address of insurance company: _____

_____

Insurance company's (or self-insured employer's) claim number: _____

Details of injury or occupational disease: _____

_____

_____

Duration of payments: _____

In addition to the above, I have received the following serious injuries, or occupational diseases, during the course of my employment:

_____

_____

All papers related to my Workmen's Compensation claims are located: _____

_____

_____

PENSIONS

My Other Benefits

☐   I do not have any pension rights.

☐   I have certain pension rights.

Name of payor: _____

Address of payor: _____

_____

Pension Identification Number: _____

There ☐ are; or, ☐ are not benefits under the plan to certain survivors upon my death.

❖❖❖❖❖❖

Name of payor: _____

Address of payor: _____

_____

_____

Pension Identification Number: _____

There ☐ are; or, ☐ are not benefits under the plan to certain survivors upon my death.

❖❖❖❖❖❖

I ☐ have; or, ☐ do not have an Individual Retirement Account (IRA).

Name of institution: _____

Address: _____

_____

IRA Account Number: _____

❖❖❖❖❖❖

I ☐ have; or, ☐ do not have a Keogh pension plan.

Name of institution: _____

Address: _____

_____

Keogh Account Number: _____

Since post-Depression deposits have been insured against bank failure by the U.S. government, Americans have pulled their money back out of cookie jars and put much of it into various financial institutions. These organizations provide places to deposit money for safekeeping, for check drafting convenience and for earning interest on certain types of accounts. In return for these and other services, the institution has the use of the money for loans and investments.

COMMERCIAL BANKS

Commercial banks offer the widest range of services among financial institutions. They handle savings and checking accounts, make a wide range of short and long term loans for personal and business use, and many provide estate and investment services.

provide estate and investment services.

Savings accounts are considered *demand deposits*. A depositor has the right to "demand," or to withdraw, any or all of his funds at any time during regular banking hours. Savings accounts bear interest which is noted, along with deposits and withdrawals, in a passbook, or savings account book. To withdraw money from an account, a depositor visits his bank and prepares a withdrawal slip. After proper identification of the depositor and updating of his passbook, the depositor receives his money. The Money Market Savings Account pays a higher rate of interest, but requires a certain minimum balance.

Checking accounts are also demand deposits, but they allow the depositor to draw checks payable to anyone. Although checking accounts historically have not paid interest, and, in fact, have often had fees charged for that service, there has been a recent change in paying interest on certain accounts.

Certificates of deposit and *money market certificates* are *time deposits*. The customer agrees to leave his money in the bank for a certain period of time — for example, two years. During this two year period, the depositor may not withdraw the funds without incurring significant interest penalties. In return for this long-term use of the depositor's money, the bank pays a higher rate of interest.

Any of the above accounts may be established in the name of a single depositor or may be owned jointly by several depositors with right of survivorship. With joint ownership, the account belongs to the survivors upon the death of one of the co-owners.

The maximum interest rates on many types of interest-bearing accounts are regulated by law and are identical at competitive banks. (A federal law adopted in 1980 gradually raises the allowable interest rate and removes all control at the end of six years.) Factors which do affect your interest return are the bank's methods of compounding interest and of crediting funds entered and withdrawn during the quarter.

For many years it was usual for banks to compound interest on a quarterly basis. Now, many banks compound interest daily in order to maximize the return they can offer.

As for the methods of crediting funds in your account, you should know whether the bank considers the first funds you deposit to be the first withdrawn (called FIFO — first in, first out), or if the last deposits are the first withdrawn (LIFO), or if your interest is paid on your low balance of the quarter. Without going into great detail, it is noteworthy that LIFO and a method called "day of deposit, day of withdrawal" (DD/DW) offer advantages to the depositor. Low balance and FIFO accounting methods may provide less interest on otherwise identical accounts, depending upon the activity in the account during the quarter.

Most banks insure their deposits through the Federal Deposit Insurance Corporation. This governmental agency was established to protect people from losing their deposited assets if a bank fails. The amount of coverage is established by law. Be sure your bank provides this insurance and check the coverage limits. Accounts can be established in several name combinations (for example, husband alone, husband and wife, wife alone, husband and child, etc.) or, if necessary, in several banks to have all of your funds insured.

MUTUAL SAVINGS BANKS

Mutual savings banks are chartered in fewer than half of the states, mostly in the Northeast, and maintain about one-fifth of the nation's savings funds. These banks specialize in mortgage and home improvement loans. Until the Federal regulations expire, mutual savings banks are allowed by law to pay a somewhat higher interest rate on savings accounts than commercial banks.

SAVINGS & LOAN ASSOCIATIONS

A savings and loan association, or building and loan association, is a group of people who have pooled their funds in order to lend money. The money is primarily loaned for home buying and building and for other construction purposes. The funds may be loaned to other members of the organization, or to non-members.

Each investor in an S&L, as they are called, is issued a number of shares in the organization, according to the amount of money invested. The dividends earned by shareholders in S&L's are similar to interest earned by depositors in a bank. Most savings and loan associations have their shares insured by the Federal Savings & Loan Insurance Corporation (FSLIC).

Although withdrawals may be limited by time savings arrangements and occasional fine print restrictions, a member of a savings and loan association is generally able to withdraw funds from his account at any time. While the association may not provide true checking accounts, a member may obtain a draft payable to another party at the time of a withdrawal or may draw on a NOW account.

The S & L's provide, basically, the same accounts as a commercial bank.

CREDIT UNIONS

A credit union is similar in nature and function to a savings and loan association. Credit union members, though, have some common bond for membership — they are employees of the same company, members of the same church, labor union, farm group, etc. Members put their money into "share accounts" and receive shares in the union. The funds are used to make short term loans to the membership.

Most credit unions honor drafts of their members. These are similar to bank checks.

SAFE-DEPOSIT BOXES

Safe-deposit boxes provide a place for the storage of valuables at a small cost. Most banks rent safe-deposit boxes. There are also a few safe-deposit companies which provide this service as their only business.

Safe-deposit boxes come in various sizes which determine the rental price. For a nominal fee, stocks, bonds, Wills, deeds, gold, silver, and other valuables can be protected from both burglary and fire. Even though this book provides document pockets for keeping valuable papers and documents, it is suggested that originals be kept in a safe-deposit box and that copies, for easy reference, be kept in this book.

When you rent a safe-deposit box, you are given a key. When you wish access to the box, both your key and a bank key must be used simultaneously. Neither key, alone, will open the box.

For further protection, you must sign a slip each time you seek access to the box. Your signature is compared to the signature placed on file at the time of the box rental.

The safe-deposit box, like a bank account, may be owned in a single name or jointly. Joint ownership allows access by someone else if you are prevented by sickness or absence, from getting into the box. In addition, joint ownership will allow access to the box by your co-owners after your death. Most states require the depository to seal the box upon learning of the death of a co-owner. However, it can be opened by a surviving co-owner in the presence of a State official who inventories the assets and delivers the inventory to the Probate Court. This assures that the assets of the decedent will be properly reported to the court and that the applicable inheritance taxes will be applied to the contents of the box.

It is most important that someone know where the key to the box is located. The forms at the end of this Chapter provide a place for you to give that information.

ACCOUNTS & SAFE-DEPOSIT BOXES

My Banking & Savings

Types of Accounts:

S – Savings Account   *C – Checking Account*   *CD – Certificate of Deposit*

MMC – Money Market Certificate

Name of institution: _____

Address: _____

_____

Account #: _____ Type: _____ Owner(s): _____

Account #: _____ Type: _____ Owner(s): _____

Account #: _____ Type: _____ Owner(s): _____

Safe-Deposit Box # _____ Key is located: _____

❖❖❖❖❖

Name of institution: _____

Address: _____

_____

Account #: _____ Type: _____ Owner(s): _____

Account #: _____ Type: _____ Owner(s): _____

Account #: _____ Type: _____ Owner(s): _____

Safe-Deposit Box # _____ Key is located: _____

❖❖❖❖❖

Name of institution: _____

Address: _____

_____

Account #: _____ Type: _____ Owner(s): _____

Account #: _____ Type: _____ Owner(s): _____

Account #: _____ Type: _____ Owner(s): _____

Safe-Deposit Box # _____ Key is located: _____

ACCOUNTS & SAFE-DEPOSIT BOXES

My Banking & Savings

Types of Accounts:

S – Savings Account   *C – Checking Account*   *CD – Certificate of Deposit*
MMC – Money Market Certificate

Name of institution:_____

Address: _____

_____

Account #:_____ Type:_____ Owner(s):_____

Account #:_____ Type:_____ Owner(s):_____

Account #:_____ Type:_____ Owner(s):_____

Safe-Deposit Box #_____ Key is located:_____

❖❖❖❖❖❖

Name of institution:_____

Address: _____

_____

Account #:_____ Type:_____ Owner(s):_____

Account #:_____ Type:_____ Owner(s):_____

Account #:_____ Type:_____ Owner(s):_____

Safe-Deposit Box #_____ Key is located:_____

❖❖❖❖❖❖

Name of institution:_____

Address: _____

_____

Account #:_____ Type:_____ Owner(s):_____

Account #:_____ Type:_____ Owner(s):_____

Account #:_____ Type:_____ Owner(s):_____

Safe-Deposit Box #_____ Key is located:_____

SAFE-DEPOSIT BOXES

My Banking & Savings

Safe-deposit box #_____ inventory:

_____

_____

_____

_____

_____

_____

_____

_____

_____

_____

_____

_____

_____

_____

_____

_____

_____

_____

_____

_____

Safe-deposit box #_____ inventory:

_____

_____

_____

_____

_____

_____

_____

_____

_____

_____

_____

_____

_____

_____

_____

_____

_____

_____

_____

_____

The term "securities," as used in this book, refers to the types of investments commonly traded on various stock exchanges or in the Over the Counter Market. They are normally handled through a stockbroker. Current exchange methods allow an investor to complete transactions almost instantaneously, making the purchase and sale of such securities a simple procedure.

STOCKS

A share of stock represents one unit of ownership in a corporation. Naturally, the percentage of ownership represented by one share of stock will depend upon the number of shares issued by the corporation. If only one hundred shares of stock are issued, one share represents a one percent ownership interest in the corporation. There may be millions of shares issued making one share of stock represent only a miniscule ownership interest.

Common stock is the basic corporate stock. If the corporation issues no other types of stock, common stock represents the entire corporate ownership. If a corporation were to dissolve, the assets (after payment of debts) would be distributed to the common stockholders in proportion to the number of shares they hold. The common stockholders have the right to manage the affairs of the corporation through a board of directors which they elect.

Preferred stock, as its name implies, has certain preferences over common stock. Many corporations do not have preferred stock. It may be established in the corporate charter when the corporation is formed, or later added to the charter by the majority action of the common stockholders.

The preferences, or priorities, given to preferred stocks are not identical within different corporations, but are spelled out in the individual corporate charters. The most usual preference enjoyed by the preferred stockholder is a priority in the distribution of profits. For example, preferred stockholders may be entitled to a fixed dividend before any dividends can be paid to common stockholders. Although this is often the only priority given to preferred stockholders, some have a preference over common stockholders in the distribution of assets when a corporation dissolves. If that is the case, the preferred stockholder is completely paid off before any distribution is made to the common stockholders.

In order to gain these preferences, preferred stockholders lose certain rights. For example, they usually do not have the right to vote for the election of the management team nor the right to share in corporate profits for any more than their fixed preferential dividends.

Since the return remains constant, the price fluctuations of preferred stock more closely resemble the price changes of corporate bonds than of common stock.

BONDS AND DEBENTURES

Most corporations need to borrow money from time to time. This may be due to cyclical money shortages, plans to expand facilities, to develop new products or for any number of other reasons. Money may either be borrowed from a lending institution, or the corporation may sell a series of bonds to investment bankers (called "underwriters") who in turn sell the bonds to investors.

There are various types of bonds issued by corporations. The simplest form of a bond is called a *debenture*. It is a form of promissory note secured only by the financial ability of the corporation to pay it when it becomes due. Along with preferred stocks, debentures are sometimes referred to as the "senior securities" of the corporation. They are entitled to interest payments before any dividends are paid on common stock, and they stand ahead of common stock in the distribution of capital if the corporation is dissolved.

When a corporation issues *mortgage bonds*, it uses certain designated assets of the corporation as security. If the company is unable to pay off the bonds when they become due, the bond holders have a priority claim against those assets. The corporation may also secure an issue of bonds by depositing certain collateral (usually stocks, bonds, etc.) with a trustee. A bond secured in this manner is called a *collateral trust bond*.

Income bonds promise to repay the principal on a designated date, but agree to pay interest only if the corporate earnings are sufficient.

Municipal bonds are issued by a state, county, city, bridge authority, or other political subdivision. Normally, they have the added advantage of being free from U.S. Federal Income Tax liability. This produces a large market in "municipals."

We normally think of a bond as being in the face amount of $1,000. However, many bonds are issued for larger or smaller amounts. Interest rates vary greatly. Some bonds may carry interest as low as 1½% or 2%, while other bonds may bring 15% or more. Since the interest rate on a bond is fixed at the time of its issue, the saleable value of the bond will rise or fall depending upon the actual rate of interest offered in the financial community. If the going interest rate is 9%, a $1,000 bond bearing 6% interest will not find a market and will have to sell for less. In reverse, if the bond bears a higher interest rate than the current rate in the financial community, it may sell for a premium.

The price of municipal and corporate bonds appearing in your newspaper reflects a percent of the face value of the bond. For example, if the face value of the bond is $1,000, a quotation of 95 means that the bond is being sold for $950. On the other hand, a quotation of 104 means the bond is being sold for $1,040. Quotations on government bonds are in decimals with the figures after the decimal point representing, curiously enough, 32nds of a dollar. A quote of 96.16 is equivalent to 96 16/32nds, or 96½, which would mean a bond with a face value of $1,000 would sell for $965.

MUTUAL FUNDS

Since some individuals do not have the confidence, the necessary "know-how," nor the desire to learn to invest their money themselves, *mutual funds* have been developed. A mutual fund acquires a portfolio of securities through the mass purchasing power of many individuals. It is managed by professionals. By selecting a mutual fund which purchases investments designed for your particular investment objectives, you get the benefits of professional management.

There are many types of mutual funds available. They may invest in common stocks specifically for income, growth, or speculative purposes. Other funds limit their purchases to municipal bonds.

Regardless of the type of mutual fund chosen, you should know that certain funds are sold by stockbrokers or salespersons and that there is an initial charge or "load" for advising you and acting as your agent. On the other hand, there are "no-load" mutual funds available through direct mailings and magazine and newspaper advertisements. A "management fee" is charged annually. This fee is usually larger for the "no-load" funds. If both "load" and "no-load" funds are held for a few years, the total cost to the investor is about the same.

MONEY MARKET FUNDS

Money market funds have recently been added to the list of securities obtainable through your stockbroker. A *money market fund* is similar to a mutual fund in that the individual's investment is combined with other investments in order to create a large fund of money which is invested in commercial paper, certificates of deposit, and other short term securities bearing high interest rates. Normally, the earnings are determined daily and interest continuously added to the investor's account. No specific rate of interest is provided (as contrasted to a bond), and the earnings fluctuate with the performance of investments in the fund. The short maturity and diversity of investment is such that, normally, there is little fluctuation in earnings over a six month period. However, the investor should continually check the performance of the fund so that money may be withdrawn if it appears that a change of investment would be advantageous.

Money market funds may be considered a parking place for money awaiting permanent investment. They provide relative safety of principal and a fairly high return of interest.

COMMODITIES

The commodities market is based upon the paper sale, or purchase, of gold, pork bellies, corn, wheat or other tangible goods for delivery on a specified date in the future. For example, if you agree to deliver a certain quantity of pork bellies in six months for $1,000, and in six months the price has dropped to $920 for that quantity, you can pick them up for $920 and deliver them at an $80 profit. If the price rises during those six months, though, you lose money.

Dealing in commodity futures is too highly speculative for the average investor. Although transactions require relatively small down payments, large profits or losses can occur. Regardless how thoroughly familiar you are with the commodities market, any investments in commodities should be regarded as very speculative.

STOCKBROKERS

Stockbrokers are in the business of handling your securities investments. You can expect them to work with you to obtain your own investment objectives — current income, long term growth, preservation of capital, or a combination of these. They act as your agent to buy, or sell, stocks and bonds, and to provide records of purchases and sales. They give you the benefit of their knowledge of investments. For these services, you pay a fee based upon the size of the transaction.

A reliable stockbroker is an invaluable ally to help you acquire and manage your investment portfolio. Unless you have the time and ability to scrutinize the performance of the many corporations on the market, you will generally be much better off to rely upon the advice of the stockbroker. Large brokerage houses have staffs which analyze the performance and potential of various stocks.

When an account with a stockbroker is established, arrangements can be made for the stocks to be retained by the brokerage. In this way, your dividends and interest are collected for you and sent to you as you wish. There is usually a small semi-annual charge for this service, but the convenience, plus the monthly and quarterly statements, are helpful in record keeping and tax preparation. They are safe and your safe deposit box will not be cluttered.

The forms at the end of this chapter provide a convenient place for you to record information about the securities you own, where they are located, and the name and address of your broker. Keep the listing of securities up to date. When you add or delete securities from the list, or even when you review the list, erase the date at the bottom of the page and insert the new date.

SECURITIES

My Securities

☐   I do not own any securities (stocks, bonds, debentures, mutual funds, etc.)

☐   I owned the securities listed on the next page as of the date the page was last revised.

☐   I have used the following brokerage firms (BR) for the purchase and sale of securities:

BR #1

Name of firm:_____ Branch:_____

Address: _____Tel.#_____

_____

_____

Account #: _____ Account Executive:_____

BR #2

Name of firm: _____ Branch: _____

Address: _____ Tel. #_____

_____

_____

Account #: _____ Account Executive: _____

BR #3

Name of firm:_____ Branch: _____

Address: _____ Tel. #_____

_____

_____

Account #:_____ Account Executive:_____

Circle "All of" or "Part of" where appropriate.

☐   **All of / Part of** my securities are kept in my safe deposit box.

☐   **All of / Part of** my securities are kept by ☐ BR #1; ☐ BR #2; ☐ BR #3.

☐   **All of / Part of** my securities are located:_____

STOCKS, BONDS, DEBENTURES & MUTUAL FUNDS

My Securities

C – Common Stock   P – Preferred Stock   M – Mutual Fund   B – Bond   D – Debenture   MMF – Money Market Funds

Company	Type of Security	Number of Shares	Date of Purchase	Total Cost Basis	Unit Basis	Adjustment to Unit Basis (Explain)

The above list of securities was last reviewed, or revised, by me on: _____ *Date*

STOCKS, BONDS, DEBENTURES & MUTUAL FUNDS

C – Common Stock   P – Preferred Stock   M – Mutual Fund   B – Bond   D – Debenture   MMF – Money Market Funds

My Securities

Company	Type of Security	Number of Shares	Date of Purchase	Total Cost Basis	Unit Basis	Adjustment to Unit Basis (Explain)

The above list of securities was last reviewed, or revised, by me on:_____

Date

STOCKS, BONDS, DEBENTURES & MUTUAL FUNDS

My Securities

C – Common Stock   P – Preferred Stock   M – Mutual Fund   B – Bond   D – Debenture   MMF – Money Market Funds

Company	Type of Security	Number of Shares	Date of Purchase	Total Cost Basis	Unit Basis	Adjustment to Unit Basis (Explain)

The above list of securities was last reviewed, or revised, by me on: _____
                                                                        Date

Real estate (or real property) is land and everything permanently attached to the land. A person buying real estate not only purchases soil, but the trees, shrubs, fences and buildings secured to it. Your house is real estate.

OWNERSHIP INTERESTS IN REAL ESTATE

The largest ownership interest available in land is called a *fee simple estate.* It provides the owner with complete control over the land — subject, of course, to zoning laws, chain of title restrictions, use of the land so that it does not interfere with adjoining property owners, etc. A fee simple estate is the type of ownership interest which is normally purchased and sold on the open market. Its name dates back to the early common law of England.

Although the common law provided for other types of estates, or interests, in land (fee simple conditional, fee tail, etc.), the only other commonly-used ownership interest is the *life estate.* A life estate, created by deed or by Will, gives a person the right to the use of the property during that person's lifetime, or during the term of some other person's life. A son, for example, may deed his mother a life estate to a home. This would insure that the mother has a place to live during her lifetime. However, upon her death, the full ownership of the property would revert to the son.

Real estate may be owned by one or by several individuals. If an individual is deeded a fee simple estate to the land, he has acquired the full ownership interest. He, alone, has the right to sell the real estate, transfer it by Will, rent it, or use it in any other legal way.

When a fee simple estate is acquired by more than one individual, however, the deed establishes whether they are *joint owners* or *common owners.* Many sorts of property may be owned through these types of ownership — automobiles, stocks, bank accounts, real estate, etc. — and there are distinct differences between the two.

With both joint and common ownership, the owners have equal rights to use and enjoy the property during their lifetimes. Joint ownership, however, includes the *right of survivorship.* When a joint owner dies, the ownership of the property remains with the surviving owner(s). The last surviving joint owner ends up as the sole owner of the property. Another feature of joint ownership is that an owner cannot sell his interest unless the other joint owner(s) join in the sale.

It is common for husband and wife to own real estate jointly as survivorship property. This avoids the necessity of probating the real estate when the first member of the marriage dies. However, survivorship property in real estate (as well as in bank accounts, etc.) could defeat the purpose of a tax saving estate plan. Before entering into any survivorship property arrangement, discuss it with your estate planner.

A surviving parent sometimes attempts to avoid probate costs by establishing joint ownership of real estate with his children. This can create a number of problems (see Chapter 8) and is not normally recommended.

With common ownership, each person owns an undivided interest in the whole property, but there is no survivorship feature. Each of the owners may sell his undivided interest or may will it on his death to whomever he wishes. When friends join together to purchase resort property for general use by their families, they often take title as common owners. If one of the owners dies, his estate, or heirs, would own his undivided interest in the real estate.

In California and a few other States, property acquired during marriage automatically becomes "community property," as long as the spouses have no agreement to the contrary. Each spouse owns a 50% interest in all such property (unless it can be shown that the property was acquired exclusively through the means of one spouse from before the marriage). As with common ownership, each spouse has the right to assign by Will the ownership of their portion of community property. If you live in a community property State, this will affect the property over which you have control in your Will.

❖❖❖❖❖

The forms in this chapter provide a place for you to list your ownership interests in real estate. It is not necessary to give the legal description of the real estate as it appears on the deed, but the land should be sufficiently identified so that it can be easily located. The deed by which you took title should be recorded at the county seat to give notice of your ownership interest in the land. After the deed has been copied by the county office, it can be placed in your files.

OWNERSHIP INTERESTS

My Real Estate

CM – Commercial   CO – Condominium   F – Farm land   I – Investment Property
O – Other (describe)   R – Residence   V – Vacant land
(The above abbreviations may be used alone or in combination to describe different types of real estate.)

☐   I have no ownership interest in any real estate.

☐   I have an ownership interest in the following real estate:

Street Address: _____

in the _____ of _____,
          Specify whether City or Township   *Name of City or Township*

County of _____ , State of _____.

Type of real estate: _____
              (R; V; CO; R/F; etc.)

My ownership interest is: ☐ sole; ☐ joint with right of survivorship with: _____

_____

☐   as a tenant in common with: _____

I acquired my ownership interest on or about: _____

My ownership interest became joint with right of survivorship on or about _____

Purchase price of real estate: _____

I owe money on the real estate to:

    Name: _____

    Address: _____

                  _____

On or about _____, I sold my ownership interest to:

    Name: _____

    Address: _____

                  _____

for the sum of $ _____ , and I receive the sum of $ _____
per month from the sale price.

The deed, land contract, mortgage, purchase information, sale information, etc., are located:

_____

OWNERSHIP INTERESTS

My Real Estate

CM – Commercial   CO – Condominium   F – Farm land   I – Investment Property
O – Other (describe)   R – Residence   V – Vacant land
(The above abbreviations may be used alone or in combination to describe different types of real estate.)

☐   I have no ownership interest in any real estate.

☐   I have an ownership interest in the following real estate:

Street Address: _____

in the _____ of _____,
      Specify whether City or Township   *Name of City or Township*

County of _____, State of _____.

Type of real estate: _____
      (R; V; CO; R/F; etc.)

My ownership interest is: ☐ sole; ☐ joint with right of survivorship with: _____

_____

☐   as a tenant in common with: _____

I acquired my ownership interest on or about: _____

My ownership interest became joint with right of survivorship on or about _____

Purchase price of real estate: _____

I owe money on the real estate to:

    Name: _____

    Address: _____

    _____

On or about _____, I sold my ownership interest to:

    Name: _____

    Address: _____

    _____

for the sum of $ _____ , and I receive the sum of $ _____
per month from the sale price.

The deed, land contract, mortgage, purchase information, sale information, etc., are located:

_____

OWNERSHIP INTERESTS

My Real Estate

CM – Commercial   CO – Condominium   F – Farm land   I – Investment Property
O – Other (describe)   R – Residence   V – Vacant land
(The above abbreviations may be used alone or in combination to describe different types of real estate.)

☐   I have no ownership interest in any real estate.

☐   I have an ownership interest in the following real estate:

Street Address: _____

in the _____ of _____ ,
Specify whether City or Township   *Name of City or Township*

County of _____ , State of _____ .

Type of real estate: _____
(R; V; CO; R/F; etc.)

My ownership interest is: ☐ sole; ☐ joint with right of survivorship with: _____

_____

☐   as a tenant in common with: _____

I acquired my ownership interest on or about: _____

My ownership interest became joint with right of survivorship on or about _____

Purchase price of real estate: _____

I owe money on the real estate to:

Name: _____

Address: _____

_____

On or about _____ , I sold my ownership interest to:

Name: _____

Address: _____

_____

for the sum of $ _____ , and I receive the sum of $ _____
per month from the sale price.

The deed, land contract, mortgage, purchase information, sale information, etc., are located:

_____

OWNERSHIP INTERESTS

My Real Estate

CM – Commercial   CO – Condominium   F – Farm land   I – Investment Property
O – Other (describe)   R – Residence   V – Vacant land
(The above abbreviations may be used alone or in combination to describe different types of real estate.)

☐   I have no ownership interest in any real estate.

☐   I have an ownership interest in the following real estate:

Street Address: _____

in the _____ of _____,
　　　　　　City or Township　　　　　　　　　　*Name of City or Township*

County of _____, State of _____.

Type of real estate: _____
　　　　　　　　　(R; V; CO; R/F; etc.)

My ownership interest is: ☐ sole; ☐ joint with right of survivorship with: _____

_____

☐   as a tenant in common with: _____

I acquired my ownership interest on or about: _____

My ownership interest became joint with right of survivorship on or about _____

Purchase price of real estate: _____

I owe money on the real estate to:

Name:　_____

Address:　_____

_____

On or about _____, I sold my ownership interest to:

Name:　_____

Address:　_____

_____

for the sum of $_____ , and I receive the sum of $_____
per month from the sale price.

The deed, land contract, mortgage, purchase information, sale information, etc., are located:

_____

The preceding Chapters provided forms for you to list your checking and savings accounts, life insurance, liability insurance, stocks, bonds, real estate, etc. This Chapter is included to provide you with forms to list your miscellaneous assets and debts.

ASSETS

Since forms cannot be tailor-made to cover the assets of everyone, this section provides a place to list a number of common assets — motor vehicles, names and addresses of debtors, business interests, whether or not you are beneficiary of a trust, whether you have an interest in a trust or real estate at the death of another person, and information regarding any claims or law suits which you may have against other persons.

Additional space is provided for you to list any other assets of value. Normally, it should not be necessary to list your household furnishings since they are out in the open for your heirs to see. However, if there is some item of furniture which has great value because of its antiquity, list it. The same applies to expensive paintings, coin or stamp collections, valuable jewelry, etc.

Have you loaned furniture to a friend, relative or to your office? Are any of the furnishings in your home borrowed from a friend? Have you already given an item to someone even though the item is still in your possession?

If there is any question as to whether a particular item should be listed, list it.

DEBTS

It is likely that your heirs will have no knowledge of your debts. Naturally, you should not take time to list monthly bills. But if you have borrowed money from a relative, friend or associate, tell your heirs about it. If someone has started a lawsuit against you, describe it and record the name of your lawyer.

My Miscellaneous Assets & Debts

☐   I own the following motor vehicles and the titles are located: _____

_____

Year	Description	Balance owed to:

The following persons owe me money:

Name of debtor	Address	Amount

☐   I have the following miscellaneous assets which might be difficult for my heirs to locate, or which might not be recognized as having significant value:

Description	Location	Significance	Estimated Value

(Any of the above may be continued on page 112)

My Miscellaneous Assets & Debts

☐ I have no ownership interest in any business.

☐ I have an interest in the following business(es):

Business Name: _____ Type of Business: _____

Address: _____ % of Ownership: _____

Partner(s): _____ % of Ownership: _____

_____ _____

_____ _____

❖❖❖❖❖❖

Business Name: _____ Type of Business: _____

Address: _____ % of Ownership: _____

Partner(s): _____ % of Ownership: _____

_____ _____

_____ _____

❖❖❖❖❖❖

Business Name: _____ Type of Business: _____

Address: _____ % of Ownership: _____

Partner(s): _____ % of Ownership: _____

_____ _____

_____ _____

❖❖❖❖❖❖

☐ I have an interest in the following patents and/or copyrights:

Description	Pending?	Date Granted	Patent or Copyright Number	Termination Date

(Any of the above may be continued on page 112.)

My Miscellaneous Assets & Debts

☐ I have a possible claim (personal injury, breach of contract, etc.) against:

Name: _____

Address: _____

_____

Description: _____

☐ I have a lawsuit pending against:

Name: _____

Address: _____

_____

☐ I have an uncollected legal judgment against: _____

Name: _____

Address: _____

_____

If you are not represented in the above by the lawyer listed in the last chapter under "Professional Advisors," list your lawyer's name and address here:

Lawyer's name: _____

Address: _____

_____

❖❖❖❖❖❖

☐ I am the beneficiary of a trust.

Description: _____

Trustee: _____

☐ I am entitled to a remainder interest in a trust or in real estate at the death of:

_____

Description: _____

Trustee (if applicable): _____

(Any of the above may be continued on page 112.)

DEBTS

My Miscellaneous Assets & Debts

☐ I owe the following debts which have not been previously mentioned:
(Personal loans, notes, etc. and NOT normal monthly bills, etc.)

To Whom	Address	What For	Amount

❖❖❖❖❖❖

(Any of the following may be continued on reverse.)

☐ I may be subject to a claim against me by: _____

Description: _____

☐ I have a pending lawsuit against me by: _____

Description: _____

☐ I have an unpaid legal judgment against me in favor of: _____

_____

Description: _____

☐ I have the following miscellaneous obligations, or debts:

Description: _____

_____

_____

_____

ASSETS & DEBTS

My Miscellaneous Assets & Debts

_____

_____

_____

_____

_____

_____

_____

_____

_____

_____

_____

_____

_____

_____

_____

_____

_____

_____

_____

_____

_____

_____

_____

The word "estate" brings to mind mansions, objets d'art, chauffeur-driven automobiles and MONEY. But do not be fooled. Anyone with a home, car, bank account, clothes, investments, or even the inherited gold watch from Grandad, has an estate. Your "estate" is the sum total of everything you own.

When a person dies, the assets in his estate are determined, the funeral expenses and other debts are paid, inheritance and estate taxes are settled and any monies owed to the person are collected. After that, the remainder is distributed according to the directions expressed in the person's Will. If there is no Will, the assets are distributed according to the laws of the State in which the person lived. One who leaves a Will is said to have died "testate" (leaving a Testament — another word for Will). A person who does not leave a Will is said to have died "intestate" (without leaving a Testament).

PROBATE

Probate is the term used for the legal procedure established by each of the States which leads to the estate's final distribution. The probate of an estate is supervised by a special court usually known as a Probate Court, or, in some States, a Surrogate Court or Orphan's Court.

Many believe that it is not necessary for an estate to be probated if the person who died, the *decedent,* has left a Will. This is not true. Some legal authority must determine its validity, identify the heirs, pass judgment on claims against the estate, calculate the amount of death taxes to be paid, and distribute the remaining assets to the proper persons. Except for determining the validity of the Will, the same procedure is followed for someone who dies intestate.

Filing fees, advertising expenses, appraiser's fees, etc., are minor costs which are involved in probating an estate. The major costs are in attorney fees and fees for the personal representative charged with the management of the estate.

EXECUTORS AND ADMINISTRATORS

If the decedent left a Will, the estate's personal representative is called an *Executor* (*Executrix* for a female), since that person "executes" the provisions of the Will. An intestate estate is "administered" by an *Administrator* (*Administratrix*). The duties are identical; only the titles differ.

The personal representative is responsible for a number of tasks. He or she must collect the assets of the decedent; have them appraised; liquidate them to pay debts or to make distribution to heirs; pay the proper claims against the estate; prepare final income tax returns for the decedent; prepare state and federal inheritance and estate tax returns; distribute the remaining assets according to the terms of the Will or the intestate laws of the state; record the necessary papers to clear title to real estate; and obtain receipts from the beneficiaries. After the receipts have been filed, the personal representative is discharged by the Probate Court.

The attorney for the estate guides the personal representative, prepares all legal Petitions, Orders, etc., and makes certain that the probate proceedings are proper.

In many States, compensation for the Executor or Administrator is set as a percentage of the inventory value of the estate. This fee is usually based upon a sliding scale. As the size of the estate increases, a smaller percentage is taken from the greater portions of the estate. For example, a personal representative might be entitled to a fee of 5% of the first $5,000 of an estate, 4% of the next $10,000, 3% of the next $35,000 and 2% of anything over $50,000.

Other States do not use a percentage figure but set the compensation in an amount which a Probate Judge has decided to be "just and reasonable." There can be a great difference in the amount of work involved by two personal representatives, even though each of the estates they handle has a value of $100,000. Clearly it would be much simpler to administer an estate consisting of $100,000 cash, with no claims against it, than to administer an estate of $100,000 with real estate, stocks, bonds, and having many debts which must be investigated and paid. Completion of the forms in this book could save fees in the probating of your estate.

ESTATE AND INHERITANCE TAXES

As part of the probate procedure, the personal representative of the estate must pay all estate and inheritance taxes due to the state and federal governments. Almost all of the States in the U.S. have some type of death tax — either an inheritance tax or an estate tax. An "inheritance tax" is based upon the amount of *inheritance* received by each beneficiary. An "estate tax" is imposed upon the total size of the *estate,* regardless of the size of the individual inheritances.

Before determining the amount of an inheritance tax or an estate tax, the laws usually provide that funeral expenses, valid debts and lawful expenses of administering the estate may first be deducted. In addition, the tax rates and exemptions imposed upon different beneficiaries may vary depending upon their kinship to the decedent. For example, a spouse may have a $30,000 exemption on an inheritance before the application of any inheritance tax. Parents, children and grandchildren may have an exemption of $5,000. However, nieces, nephews, aunts, uncles, cousins and non-relatives may have no exemption. Then, for example, spouses, children, parents and grandchildren may pay a rate of 2% on the first $50,000 inherited, 4% on the next $100,000, 6% on the next $300,000, etc. At the same time, all other persons may be taxed at 10% on the first $50,000, 12% on the next $100,000, and so forth. Usually, charitable gifts are not taxed so long as the recipient qualifies as a true, charitable organization.

With estate taxes, just like federal income taxes, the lowest rate is applied to the bottom portion of an estate. As an estate rises in value, the tax rate increases, in stairstep percentages, on the higher values.

The "taxable estate" may not be the same as the inventory value of assets set by the Probate Court. For example, even though jointly owned property is neither probated nor generally subject to State death taxes, it is considered to be part of the "taxable estate" for federal estate tax purposes. Life insurance proceeds and almost any asset which passes to another individual are also subject to federal estate taxes, whether or not the State requires probate of those assets.

In a sizeable estate, the federal estate tax can be very expensive. There are ways to minimize the taxes imposed upon your estate. *See a good estate planner.* If you do not know one, talk to your lawyer. If he has the background to plan your estate, he will. If not, he can refer you to a qualified person.

GIFTS

A person who makes a gift (a donor) is subject to the federal gift tax. However, not all gifts are taxable. Each donor is entitled to a $10,000 annual exclusion on gifts to each recipient. As of January 1, 1982, a donor can give $10,000 to as many different persons or organizations as he desires, without being subject to tax. There are other exceptions which may apply to particular gifts. They should be investigated if you intend to be a donor.

It is important that you keep a record of your gifts since the information will be needed by your personal representative for federal estate tax purposes. A place has been provided in the forms for your notations.

THE WILL

In Merrie Olde England, a person had little control over the manner in which his estate was divided. Distribution was generally determined by British law, which generously rewarded the first-born son, to the virtual exclusion of other children. It was not until 1540 A.D. that the first Statute of Wills gave a person the right to decide, to some extent, how his property should be distributed after his death.

In order to prevent forgeries, fraud and undue influence, each State has prescribed the method for a Will to be executed. Although the requirements are relatively simple, they must be strictly followed or the Will will not be valid. The State provides that the Will must be identified as such by the signer to a certain number of witnesses. Then, usually, the signer and the witnesses must sign the Will in the presence of each other. Unfortunately, many people attempt to prepare their own Wills without being aware of the formal requirements of execution. This may result in an invalid Will.

It is not worthwhile to save money by preparing your own Will. See your attorney! Discuss with him the cost of a Will and, if you feel his fee is too high, shop around. An attorney should be able to prepare the usual simple Will for a modest fee. The attorney not only knows the formal requirements for the execution of the Will, but he will be able to set out your desires clearly so that the chance of some disgruntled individual contesting the validity of the Will will be minimized.

The laws of some States recognize that there can be circumstances in which an individual may not have time to arrange for a proper Will. For example, a soldier dying on the field of battle would have no opportunity to prepare and execute a Will. In circumstances of impending death, some States will allow an oral (nuncupative) Will. Don't rely on this! In addition, some States allow an unwitnessed Will which is entirely in the handwriting of the testator (a holographic Will). Don't rely on this either!

A Will allows you to designate the beneficiaries of your estate. Generally, a man who leaves a valid Will in effect at his death (a testator) cannot exclude his wife. If he does, the wife has a right to "take against the Will" and receive a certain percentage (up to 100%) of the amount she would have received had there been no Will. In response to the changing view of women in society, some States have enacted similar provisions to protect the husband from exclusion by the wife's Will. Except for the limitations involving a spouse, a testator can generally leave his estate to anyone.

By Will, a person may, among other things, designate an executor; decide whether adopted grandchildren will inherit in the same manner as natural grandchildren; appoint a guardian of any minor children; and create a trust.

TRUST AGREEMENTS

A trust can be established in a Will (called a "testamentary trust") to accomplish many different ends. For example, a testator may have raised two of his children, at his expense, through a full college education. He may, however, have a young child at home. If his estate were left equally to his three children, it would mean that the youngster would have to provide for his own upbringing and college education out of his one-third share of the estate. To avoid this injustice, the testator could leave his estate to a trustee (a bank or trust company, for example) for the use and benefit of all of his children. However, the trustee might be instructed that no division should be made of the estate assets until the estate had paid for the upbringing and college education of the young child. Many variations can be made in the scheme of *when* inheritances should be paid, *how* they should be paid and *under what circumstances* they should be paid. In effect, the trustee handles the estate for a certain period of time after the person's death in the manner the person has directed.

Trusts can also be used by an estate planner to help minimize the effects of estate taxation. Since this can become quite involved, your particular situation should be discussed with an estate planning specialist.

Besides being established by a Will, trusts can also be created during the person's lifetime. The individual enters into a trust agreement with a selected trustee, most commonly a bank. The establishment of such a trust is generally for estate planning or tax saving purposes. Such a trust (created during lifetime) is called a "living" or "inter vivos" trust.

The individual can transfer ownership of desired assets to the trustee. At the death of the individual, the trustee will distribute the remaining assets in the trust in accordance with the provisions of the trust agreement.

The inter vivos trust may be used to avoid the probating of a decedent's assets. Whether or not this would fit your particular situation can best be determined by your estate planner.

INTESTATE SUCCESSION

If you die without a Will (intestate), your estate will be distributed in accordance with the laws of *intestate succession.* The laws of your State of residence will govern the distribution of all of your assets except real estate located in another State or country; and the laws of the State in which the real estate is located will determine its distribution. Whether you like it or not, that's the way it is!

All of the States have established laws to determine the manner of estate distribution for an intestate decedent. Without these laws, there would be endless family disputes over the decedent's worldly goods. (If you don't think this is true, any lawyer will vouch for the family fights that take place even under the laws of intestate succession.)

It is always possible that your State's laws of intestate succession will provide the exact method by which you wish to divide your estate. But don't count on it! Since most persons want everything to go to their spouse, it seems strange that the various legislatures did not design it that way. In most instances, the surviving spouse will receive 50% of the estate if there is one surviving child and 1/3 of the estate if there are two or more surviving children. On the other hand, if there are no surviving children, the spouse normally gets 50% and the parents of the decedent get 50%. If something like this is what you want, check the laws of intestate succession in the State in which you reside and in any other State in which you own real estate, and sit back and do nothing. On the other hand, if you want your assets specifically distributed according to your wishes, have your attorney prepare a Will which reflects those wishes.

JOINTLY OWNED PROPERTY

The intestate succession laws or directions of your Will affect only property that *you* own at the time of your death. Many people own real estate, bank accounts, automobiles, etc., in joint names, with right of survivorship, with their spouse or with someone else. At the death of a co-owner, joint property automatically belongs to the surviving co-owner. In other words, *joint property is not an asset of the decedent's estate.* Neither the Will nor the laws of intestate succession can control the distribution of joint property. You must take this into consideration for your after-death planning.

There are certain advantages to joint ownership in estate planning. However, a total reliance on joint ownership to effect a plan of estate distribution may end up defeating the equitable distribution that you had envisioned.

For example, let us suppose that your spouse dies before you, and that you have three adult children who, in turn, have children. In order to avoid probate expense (since jointly owned property does not require probate administration), it would appear simple to place your home in the names of yourself and each of your three children, jointly. Then, upon your death, the three children would be joint co-owners of the home. Simple? Not really. Too many things can happen. Suppose child A dies shortly after your death. Now the home is owned by children B and C — to the exclusion of child A's children. Or, suppose you subsequently decide that you wish to sell the home and one of your children, for whatever reason, refuses to approve the sale. An expensive legal proceeding could force the sale, but the unwilling child might be entitled to one-fourth of the proceeds. Or, suppose one of the children became mentally incompetent and could not join in a sale of the real estate. Then, although a guardian could be appointed to enter into the sale, the incompetent child's estate would have to receive one-fourth of the proceeds. Or, suppose you and your three children were killed in an automobile accident, but that child C died five minutes later than the other three co-owners. Under those circumstances, child C's estate would be the sole owner of the real estate since he had outlived the other joint co-owners.

As stated above, there may be a definite place for joint ownership of real estate, bank accounts, etc., in your estate planning. However, be sure that you know what you are doing and talk it over with your lawyer.

Remember, your Will does not control jointly owned property.

YOUR WILL AND LIFE INSURANCE

The beneficiaries of your life insurance are determined by the life insurance contract between you and the insurance company. Neither your Will nor the laws of intestate succession can designate to whom life insurance proceeds shall be paid. Of course, if your insurance contract designates your estate as the beneficiary of the insurance policy, the insurance company will pay the proceeds to your personal representative who, in turn, will distribute the proceeds to the estate beneficiaries.

As you can see, the execution of a Will does not cover everything. But with careful planning and professional advice, you can maximize the likelihood of having your wishes carried out exactly as you expect.

THE LIVING WILL

There are those who would prefer to die with the dignity of accepting their natural mortality than to be kept "alive" through extraordinary measures when there is little serious hope of recovery. Should this be your wish, a Living Will has been provided to express your decision to your heirs, your physicians and other concerned individuals. This is not solely for the purpose of declaring your wishes, but also to spare your survivors from facing such a decision and to offer some legal protection to medical personnel acting according to your instructions.

To make best use of your Living Will, sign and date it in front of two witnesses. Give copies to those concerned — your family, your family doctor, etc. — and discuss it with them. Since this is not a legal document, it is important that those who will be carrying out your wishes be aware of and willing to carry out your decision. Look over your Living Will yearly, and if you have not changed your thoughts about it, initial and date it.

The Living Will has been prepared by The Euthanasia Educational Fund, 250 W. 57th Street, New York, N.Y. 10019.

MY WILL

My Will, Trust Agreements, etc.

☐   I do not have a Will.

☐   I executed my Last Will and Testament on: _____

The Will was prepared by:

Name of Attorney: _____

Name of law firm: _____

Address: _____
         Street Address and Apartment Number

         City   *State*   *Zip Code*

The Will was witnessed by:

Name: _____

Address: _____
         Street Address and Apartment Number

         City   *State*   *Zip Code*

Further identification (neighbor, co-worker, etc.): _____

Name: _____

Address: _____
         Street Address and Apartment Number

         City   *State*   *Zip Code*

Further identification: _____

Name: _____

Address: _____
         Street Address and Apartment Number

         City   *State*   *Zip Code*

Further identification: _____

CODICILS, TRUSTS, POWER OF ATTORNEY

My Will, Trust Agreements, etc.

Since the Will was executed, I have executed _____ Codicils to the Will.

The Codicils were executed on the following dates: _____

Name of Personal Representative: _____

Address: _____

_____

Name of Trustee: _____

Address: _____

_____

My original Will (with Codicils) is located: _____

_____ and a copy is located:

☐ in Document Pocket #2, or ☐ _____

❖❖❖❖❖

☐   I have not executed a living Trust Agreement which is in effect at this time.

☐   I entered into a living Trust Agreement on _____with:

Name of Trustee: _____

Address: _____

_____

The original Trust Agreement is located: _____

_____ and a copy is located:

☐ in Document Pocket #2, or ☐ _____

❖❖❖❖❖

The following person is entrusted with Power of Attorney:

Name: _____

Address: _____

Effective Date: _____ Expiration Date: _____

GIFTS

My Will, Trust Agreements, etc.

☐   I have made no gifts in excess of $10,000.

☐   I have made the following gifts in excess of $10,000:

To Whom (Donee)	Date	Gift	Value

I have filed the following Federal Gift Tax returns:

Period Covered	Internal Revenue Office Where Filed

A LIVING WILL

My Will, Trust Agreements, etc.

TO MY FAMILY, MY PHYSICIAN, MY LAWYER, MY CLERGYMAN

TO ANY MEDICAL FACILITY IN WHOSE CARE I HAPPEN TO BE

TO ANY INDIVIDUAL WHO MAY BECOME RESPONSIBLE FOR MY HEALTH, WELFARE OR AFFAIRS:

Death is as much a reality as birth, growth, maturity and old age — it is the one certainty of life. If the time comes when I, _____ , can no longer take part in decisions for my own future, let this statement stand as an expression of my wishes while I am still of sound mind.

If the situation should arise in which there is no reasonable expectation of my recovery from physical or mental disability, I request that I be allowed to die and not be kept alive by artificial means or "heroic measures." I do not fear death itself as much as the indignities of deterioration, dependence and hopeless pain. I, therefore, ask that medication be mercifully administered to me to alleviate suffering even though this may hasten the moment of death.

This request is made after careful consideration. I hope you who care for me will feel morally bound to follow its mandate. I recognize that this appears to place a heavy responsibility upon you, but it is with the intention of relieving you of such responsibility and of placing it upon myself in accordance with my strong convictions, that this statement is made.

Signed _____

Date: _____

Witness: _____

Witness: _____

Copies of this request have been given to: _____

_____

_____

If you ever buried a loved one without previous discussion as to how the body should be handled, you will remember your guilt feelings as you made the funeral arrangements. Have I spent enough on this funeral? Am I showing proper respect and love for the deceased? Should the casket be open? Would cremation be preferable? Should the body be donated for medical education?

You can spare your heirs this mental anguish by making the decisions yourself. The forms in this chapter allow you to clearly state your wishes.

When a person dies, the body must be handled in some manner. This is normally done by burial in the earth, entombment, cremation or by bequeathal of the body to a medical school . This is the first determination you must make.

Your decision may be influenced by your personal wishes, your religious background, comparative costs and other factors. For many years, cremation violated the precepts of Roman Catholicism. However, a change has taken place and many Catholics accept cremation following a religious service with the remains present. Generally speaking, Jews do not accept cremation.

It is not the purpose of this book to attempt to persuade you that one method is superior to another. If you wish to spend $25,000 on your funeral, fine. That is your business. On the other hand, if you prefer the simplicity of the least expensive method, that, too, is entirely up to you. *But tell it to your heirs!*

If you choose to have a funeral, you must decide whether it is to be public or private, whether you want an open or closed casket, who is to be the funeral director, whether or not you want flowers, whether you have any preference in music, who is to be the minister, priest or rabbi, whether there should be a graveside service for the commitment of your body, whether you wish memorial donations to be made to a specific organization, and whether you wish the service to be held in a church or a funeral home. There are a lot of decisions, aren't there? To make certain your preferences are known, it is best to photocopy the completed forms in this chapter and give them to your next of kin and to the funeral director or memorial society of your choice.

BURIAL AND ENTOMBMENT

Burial in the earth is, by far, the most common method in the United States of dealing with the remains. Although early Americans usually buried a body in a family or churchyard cemetery, all of the United States now have regulations requiring burial in licensed cemeteries. The body is placed in a casket, lowered into the ground and covered with earth.

Caskets, or *coffins,* encase the corpse for burial purposes. They can vary from a simple pine box to an elaborate bronze coffin with an innerspring mattress. The cost of the casket will greatly affect the total charges for the funeral.

Vaults of concrete, or similar materials, are often used to surround the casket to help prevent water seepage and to prevent settling of the soil as a wooden coffin disintegrates.

Cemetery lots for earth burial may be purchased for individual caskets. Larger lots may be purchased for future use by an entire family. Most cemeteries now include in the sale price of the lot a charge for its perpetual care.

The *cost of cemetery lots* varies enormously. In urban areas costs are generally more than in rural areas because of the higher property value. Even in the same community, there can be wide variations of costs from one cemetery to another; and indeed, substantial differences in the same cemetery. A gravesite located on a hill, for example, may be much more expensive than a cemetery lot on lower ground.

Entombment is similar to burial in the earth except that the casket is placed in a private tomb or in a *crypt* located in a building called a *mausoleum*. Mausoleums may range from 1 to 20 stories in height. Crypts may be purchased for individual caskets or for a family of caskets.

If you choose to be buried in a cemetery or entombed in a mausoleum, you should tell your heirs where this is to take place. In other words, *select your cemetery or mausoleum*. You do not need to purchase a cemetery lot or crypt. Such a purchase is recommended, though, if you are certain that you do not intend to move from the area, or if you wish to use a specific cemetery or mausoleum regardless of future moves. Many people plan to retire to warmer climates or other desirable spots, if they can afford this luxury. If you have made a firm decision about this, purchase your lot or crypt. On the other hand, if you are not sure about your ultimate living site, merely note your preference of cemetery or mausoleum. Make sure that the cemetery of your choice allows burial without a vault, if this type of burial is your preference.

Monuments, headstones and grave markers may be used in cemeteries to identify the person buried. Monuments and headstones are generally made of stone and extend above the ground in varying heights. Grave markers are generally made of metal or stone and are placed flat on the ground. Many of the newer cemeteries require flat grave markers so that large mowing machines can operate freely. Where there are monuments or headstones, lawns must be mowed by hand — meaning higher labor costs. If you prefer a monument atop your grave, make sure that the cemetery you choose will allow it.

While you are making these decisions, you might as well determine the wording on your monument or marker. Although the majority of grave markers and monuments merely give the name of the grave occupant, the year of birth and the year of death, many monuments have epitaphs chosen by the deceased or his heirs. Note any specific directions you might have for this.

If you are a veteran of the United States military, and if your last discharge was other than dishonorable, the Veteran's Administration will furnish, upon request, a headstone or marker for your unmarked grave. In addition, you, your spouse, or minor children may be buried in any National Cemetery in which space is available. (See Chapter 5, Veteran's Benefits.)

CREMATION

Cremation is a method of disposing of a body by placing it in a special furnace which reduces it to ashes. Although less than 10% of the bodies in the United States are cremated, cremation is used widely in certain parts of the world. In fact, the word "funeral" is derived from an old word of northern India which means "smoke." Today, many people of India burn their dead on funeral pyres and scatter the ashes on the sacred river Ganges. The Vikings placed their dead in boats, set the boats afire, and sent them out to sea.

Following cremation, the ashes are returned to the heirs in a box or urn and may be scattered, buried, or placed in a niche or vault in a *columbarium.* A columbarium is a building which has been constructed for this particular purpose.

If a decision is based solely on cost, it is clear that cremation will be less expensive than burial or entombment since it will not be necessary to buy a cemetery lot or mausoleum crypt, a grave marker or monument. However, many crematoriums require that the body be placed in a casket at the time of cremation, so an inexpensive casket may be needed.

BEQUEATHAL TO A MEDICAL SCHOOL

You may desire to donate your body to medical education. All 50 States have passed the Uniform Anatomical Gift Act which allows you to give your body to medical schools or hospitals for scientific use. Many feel that this is the least costly way of handling your remains.

Since rules and regulations differ among the various medical schools, it is necessary to familiarize yourself with the requirements of a particular medical school. Some schools require embalming; others forbid it. Some pay all costs of transportation; some pay none. Those with a surplus of bodies will accept no more; others are in desperate need of donations. Individual schools will be glad to provide you with printed materials describing their requirements and telling you how to donate your body.

The medical school will arrange for the disposition of the remains following the useful educational life of the body. This will be done at no cost to the family. If the family wishes the cremated remains returned, arrangements may be made with the medical school.

DONATION OF BODY PARTS

You may want to donate certain portions of your body for use as transplants. These donations have proved invaluable to thousands of living persons. Such organs as kidneys, hearts, lungs, skin and corneas have been successfully transplanted. In the future, many other organs may prove usable.

After the parts have been removed from the deceased, the remains can be buried, entombed or cremated exactly as though the body were intact. Most medical schools will not accept your body for anatomical study if you have made a part donation (with the exception of cornea donations). You will have to choose between a body or a part donation.

UNIFORM ANATOMICAL GIFT ACT

The Uniform Anatomical Gift Act provides a method for the individual to donate his body for anatomical study, or to donate body parts for transplant, by the execution of a prescribed legal document signed by the donor and two witnesses. This document has been reduced to wallet-size in the Uniform Donor Card which can be carried by the donor. Since speed is essential for transplantation of body parts, the donor should carry the Uniform Donor Card on his person so that it is readily available if he should die as the result of an accident. The National Institutes of Health have published a pamphlet entitled "How to Donate the Body or its Organs" which gives additional information and provides you with a Uniform Donor Card. If you are interested, write to the U.S. Department of Health and Human Services, Washington, D.C., and request Publication No. (NIH) 79-776. Many States provide a Uniform Donor Card on the backs of drivers' licenses. The front and back of two Uniform Donor Cards appear on pages 133 and 134. They can be removed from the book, and carried in your wallet.

A Uniform Donor Card carried by you at the time of your death does not assure that your wishes will be followed. Even though you sign a Uniform Donor Card or other legal document, doctors are unlikely to carry out your wishes if the next-of-kin is opposed. Make sure that your next-of-kin knows your wishes and is willing to abide by them.

FUNERAL SERVICES

Funeral services consist of the observances held for a deceased person before a burial or cremation. These services may include religious rites, fraternal or military procedures, a commitment service at graveside, etc. In this book, the term "funeral services" will refer to ceremonies conducted with the body of the deceased present. If the body is not present, the last observances will be called "memorial services."

A *funeral director* is a person who, as his name implies, makes all of the funeral arrangements according to the desires of the family, notifies the newspapers, makes specific arrangements with the minister or rabbi, makes arrangements with the cemetery or crematorium and prepares the body for burial or cremation. He generally stocks an array of caskets in various price ranges so that the family may select its needs. He is generally familiar with the requirements of life insurance companies, unions, Social Security and the Veteran's Administration so that he is able to help the family file necessary papers to obtain benefits. His help can be invaluable to a bereaved family at the time of death.

The family of a deceased may be emotionally disturbed following the death of a loved one, and may, because of guilt feelings, spend much more money for the funeral than the deceased would want. Funeral directors can provide an inexpensive service, but if the bereaved wants something more expensive, it will certainly be arranged.

You can express your wishes as to the cost of the funeral by filling out the appropriate forms at the end of this chapter. Or, you can pre-arrange your own funeral with the funeral director right now. Not only can you make the specific arrangements, you can also arrange for pre-payment. Because of a history of abuses by a few members of the funeral industry, most of the States have established rules and conditions to protect the funeral investor from fraud. It is usual in many States to have the money for prepaid funeral arrangements deposited in a bank account in the joint names of the arranger and the funeral director. The funeral director cannot withdraw the money until the death of the arranger. However, the arranger can always withdraw the money and terminate the arrangements. Of course, any pre-arrangement that you make may be useless unless your heirs are aware of them.

You, or your heirs, must determine whether or not you wish your body to be *embalmed*. Embalming is the process by which blood and body fluids are removed from the corpse and a preserving fluid injected into the arteries. An embalmed body is temporarily preserved from decay. Since a decaying body could cause disease, embalming is looked upon as a health measure. It also preserves the features of the body for viewing at an open-casket funeral.

No State requires embalming if the burial or cremation occurs soon after death. If you intend to have an open casket funeral, you must, of course, opt for embalming. On the other hand, if you do not intend to let people view your body after your death, it need not be embalmed unless you so desire. Tell your heirs your wishes.

You may have specific desires as to music, or no music, at your funeral; flowers, or no flowers; certain poetry, or no poetry; military, or non-military procedures; or other specific rites. Provision is made in the forms for you to express these wishes.

MEMORIAL SERVICES

Memorial services, as the term is used in this book, are similar to funeral services, except that the body of the deceased is not present. It has been buried, cremated, sent to a medical school, or perhaps even lost in a catastrophe. It may be the wishes of the deceased or the family to deal with the remains before holding formal services. Or, a memorial service may be arranged because family and friends are unable to gather immediately after death. Memorial services, like funeral services, can be religious or non-religious in character. They can be held at a church, home, funeral home, rented hall or any other place. They are in remembrance of, and with respect for, the deceased. If you prefer a memorial service to a funeral service, let your heirs know.

MEMORIAL SOCIETIES

Memorial societies have arisen throughout the country to provide members a simple, inexpensive method of handling remains. Generally, they advocate immediate cremation (without embalmment or funeral services) followed by a memorial service commemorating the deceased. Forms are provided to the members so that they may express their preferences. At the time of death, members of the society assist the family in making arrangements. Depending upon the laws of the particular State, a memorial society may be able to go so far as to transfer the body from a hospital directly to a crematorium; or it may be restricted to giving only advice to the family.

GENERAL

My Final Wishes & Guide for Survivors

I wish my body to be:

- □ buried in the earth.
- □ entombed in a mausoleum.
- □ cremated.
- □ bequeathed to a medical school.
- □ certain body parts donated.
- □ any of the above as determined by my heirs.

I wish that there be:

- □ a funeral service (body present).
- □ a memorial service (body not present).
- □ no service.
- □ any of the above.

I wish that a funeral, or memorial, service be held at:

- □ church.
- □ funeral home.
- □ my home.
- □ other: _____
- □ any of the above.

My preferences are as follows:

Name of church, synagogue, etc.: _____

Minister, priest or rabbi: _____

Funeral home: _____

I □ am, or, □ am not a member of a Memorial Society with which I have left my wishes as to the disposition of my remains. The name, address and telephone number is:

_____

_____

_____

_____

FUNERAL OR MEMORIAL SERVICE

My Final Wishes & Guide for Survivors

I wish the service to be for: ☐ friends and relatives; ☐ private; ☐ other: _____

_____

I wish the casket to be: ☐ open; ☐ closed.

My favorite hymns/music are: _____

_____

Soloist:_____

My favorite scriptures, poems, etc., are: _____

_____

I ☐ do, or, ☐ do not wish flowers.

Disposal of flowers: _____

I am a member of the following Organization (War Veterans, Masons, etc.) and desire an Organization

    service: _____

I request that memorial contributions be made to: _____

I ☐ do, or, ☐ do not wish to be embalmed.

I ☐ do, or, ☐ do not wish to have an interment service at graveside.

I wish the expense of my funeral to be: ☐ minimal; ☐ low average; ☐ average; ☐ high average;

    ☐ not limited.

I prefer the following funeral home: _____

_____

I ☐ have, or, ☐ have not made funeral pre-arrangements with the funeral home.

I ☐ have, or, ☐ have not made any pre-payment of funeral expenses.

If I have made any pre-payment, it is as follows: _____

_____

_____

_____

_____*(Any of the above may be continued on reverse.)*

FUNERAL OR MEMORIAL SERVICE

My Final Wishes & Guide for Survivors

_____
_____
_____
_____
_____
_____
_____
_____
_____
_____
_____
_____
_____
_____
_____
_____
_____
_____
_____
_____
_____
_____
_____

BURIAL AND ENTOMBMENT

My Final Wishes & Guide for Survivors

☐   I do not own, nor have the legal use of, a cemetery lot or mausoleum crypt.

☐   I ☐ own, or, ☐ have the legal use of:

    ☐   a cemetery lot.

    ☐   a mausoleum crypt.

The ownership of the lot. or crypt, is in the name of: _____

_____

The lot, or crypt, is located at:

    Cemetery or mausoleum: _____

    Address: _____

    Section: _____ Lot # _____

    Other description: _____

    _____

    Location of deed: _____

I desire a ☐ grave marker, or, ☐ monument.

In addition to my name, date of birth and date of death, I would like the following to be placed
    thereon: _____

_____

_____

Special instructions: _____

_____

_____

_____

_____

_____

_____

_____

CREMATION

My Final Wishes & Guide for Survivors

☐　I wish my body to be cremated immediately.

☐　I wish my body to be cremated immediately and a memorial service subsequently held.

☐　I wish my body to be cremated following a funeral service.

☐　I wish my body to be cremated, but I leave the other details to my heirs.

Following my cremation, I wish my ashes:

☐　to be scattered (where permitted by law): _____

_____

☐　to be placed in an urn and buried, or entombed: _____

_____

☐　to be handled as my heirs determine.

BEQUEATHAL TO A MEDICAL SCHOOL

My Final Wishes & Guide for Survivors

☐ I wish my body to be bequeathed to:

Medical School: _____

Address: _____

_____

and/or

☐ any other medical school if inconvenient to send to the above, or, if not needed by the above.

I ☐ have, or, ☐ have not made pre-arrangements with the above Medical School.

I realize that, sometimes, the above arrangements cannot be carried out. My alternative desire is for:

   ☐   burial or entombment
   ☐   cremation

and I have filled out the pertinent portion of these forms in case an alternative to body bequeathal is necessary.

☐ I have executed a Uniform Donor Card and it is located: _____

_____

THE ABOVE BODY BEQUEST WILL NOT BE EFFECTIVE WITHOUT THE EXECUTION OF A UNIFORM DONOR CARD AND THE APPROVAL OF THE NEXT-OF-KIN.

❖❖❖❖❖

UNIFORM DONOR CARD	UNIFORM DONOR CARD
OF _____ *Print or type name of Donor* In the hope that I may help others, I hereby make this ana- tomical gift, if medically acceptable, to take effect upon my death. The words and marks below indicate my desires. I give: (a) _____ any needed organs or parts. (b) _____ only the following organs or parts: _____ *Specify the organ(s) or part(s)* for the purposes of transplantation, therapy, medical research or education. (c) _____ my body for anatomical study if needed. Limitations or special wishes, if any: _____ _____	OF _____ *Print or type name of Donor* In the hope that I may help others, I hereby make this ana- tomical gift, if medically acceptable, to take effect upon my death. The words and marks below indicate my desires. I give: (a) _____ any needed organs or parts. (b) _____ only the following organs or parts: _____ *Specify the organ(s) or part(s)* for the purposes of transplantation, therapy, medical research or education. (c) _____ my body for anatomical study if needed. Limitations or special wishes, if any: _____ _____

The Uniform Donor Cards above may be removed from the book to be carried in a wallet or purse. Both sides of a card must be completed, signed and witnessed to be valid.

DONATION OF BODY PARTS

My Final Wishes & Guide for Survivors

☐   I do not wish to donate any body parts.

☐   I wish to donate any needed body parts. *(If you are bequeathing your body to a Medical School, do not donate any parts except corneas from the eyes.)*

☐   I wish to donate only the following organs or parts:

     ☐   kidneys

     ☐   corneas from the eyes

     ☐   bone

     ☐   skin

     ☐   blood vessels

     ☐   cartilage

     ☐   other: _____

_____

☐   Limitations, or special wishes: _____

_____

_____

☐   I have executed a Uniform Donor Card and it is located: _____

_____

THE ABOVE DONATIONS WILL NOT BE EFFECTIVE WITHOUT THE EXECUTION OF A UNIFORM DONOR CARD AND THE APPROVAL OF THE NEXT-OF-KIN.

❖❖❖❖❖❖

Signed by the donor and the following two witnesses in the presence of each other.

_____   _____
Signature of Donor   *Date of Birth*

_____   _____
City & State   *Date Signed*

_____   _____
Witness   *Witness*

This is a legal document under the Uniform Anatomical Gift Act or similar laws.

Signed by the donor and the following two witnesses in the presence of each other.

_____   _____
Signature of Donor   *Date of Birth*

_____   _____
City & State   *Date Signed*

_____   _____
Witness   *Witness*

This is a legal document under the Uniform Anatomical Gift Act or similar laws.

The Uniform Donor Cards above may be removed from the book to be carried in a wallet or purse. Both sides of a card must be completed, signed and witnessed to be valid.

A GUIDE FOR MY SURVIVORS

My Final Wishes & Guide for Survivors

AT TIME OF DEATH:

Refer to the following forms:

☐   Immediately authorize donation of body parts.*   134

☐   Contact medical school for body bequeathal.*   133

☐   Contact funeral director or memorial society.   128

☐   Notify friends, relatives and employer.   136

☐   Maintain a list of flowers, cards, donations and other expressions of sympathy.

☐   Arrange for friends and relatives to help as needed with childcare,
           shopping, cooking, telephones, etc.

☐   Arrange funeral or memorial service.   129

☐   Arrange for cemetery lot, mausoleum or crypt.*   131

☐   Provide obituary information to newspaper.   4-6, 37, 39, 55-64

☐   Arrange for after-service luncheon or gathering for friends and relatives.

☐   Obtain a minimum of 8 certified copies of death certificates.

FOLLOWING FUNERAL OR MEMORIAL SERVICE:

☐   Send notes to acknowledge expressions of sympathy.

☐   Notify life insurance companies and file claim forms.   69-71

☐   Notify other insurance companies and file claims where applicable.   72-76
      —   Medical, Health, Disability, Accident & Travel   73-74
      —   Vehicle   75-76
      —   Residence   72

☐   Apply for appropriate benefits:
      —   Social Security death benefits and other applicable benefits   82
      —   Veteran's burial benefits and other applicable benefits   83
      —   Pension benefits   86
      —   Workmen's Compensation benefits   85

☐   Meet with lawyer to commence probate proceedings if needed.   119-120
      —   Take original Will and copies of forms, in this book.   119-120
      —   Assist with inventory of assets, etc.   69-71, 90-92, 97-100,
                                                103-106, 108-112

☐   Notify accountant/tax preparer (unless estate lawyer is preparing final tax returns).   138
      —   Take copies of appropriate forms in this book.   121
      —   Take copies of recent tax returns.   138

☐   Notify stockbroker.   97
      —   Change ownership of joint stocks by removing name of decedent.   98-100
      —   Suspend any open orders of the decedent.

☐   Notify banker.   90-91
      —   Change ownership of joint accounts by removing name of decedent.   90-91

☐   Cancel and destroy credit cards.   139

     * *If applicable.*

A GUIDE FOR SURVIVORS

My Final Wishes & Guide for Survivors

The following people should be contacted in the event of my death:

Name	Address	Phone	Relationship (Friend, employer, cousin, etc.)

When you have completed all of the preceding forms, there may be other information that you wish listed for your heirs. Only you know what that may be. Perhaps there are certain papers or letters that you wish destroyed without being opened. If so, tell your heirs about it.

You may wish to list your various credit cards and numbers with the names and addresses of the companies. These should be cancelled by your heirs after your death and the cards destroyed. (It may also be of great help if your wallet is lost or stolen.)

Maybe you have personal messages that you wish relayed to people after your death. Here is a place to do it.

In other words, these last forms are solely for your use as you see fit.

❖❖❖❖❖

Keep this book up to date.

Share it with your heirs.

❖❖❖❖❖

GOOD LUCK AND GOOD HEALTH!

PROFESSIONAL ADVISORS

Miscellaneous Information

My lawyer is: _____

Address: _____

_____

My accountant/tax preparer is: _____

Address: _____

_____

Copies of my income tax returns are located: _____

_____

My dentist is: _____

Address: _____

_____

My personal physician is: _____

Address: _____

_____

My specialty physician is: _____

Address: _____

_____

My specialty physician is: _____

Address: _____

_____

My specialty physician is: _____

Address: _____

_____

My_____ is: _____
      Profession

Address: _____

_____

CREDIT CARDS & MISCELLANEOUS

Miscellaneous Information

I have the following credit cards:

Name of Company	Address	Card Number

❖❖❖❖❖

Please destroy the following items without opening, or reading them: _____

_____

_____

My driver's license #: _____ Expires: _____

Passport Number: _____ Date of Issue: _____

Country of Issue: _____ Location: _____

NOTES FOR MY HEIRS

Miscellaneous Information

_____

_____

_____

_____

_____

_____

_____

_____

_____

_____

_____

_____

_____

_____

_____

_____

_____

_____

_____

_____

_____

_____

_____

NOTES FOR MY HEIRS

Miscellaneous Information

_____

_____

_____

_____

_____

_____

_____

_____

_____

_____

_____

_____

_____

_____

_____

_____

_____

_____

_____

_____

_____

_____

_____

NOTES FOR MY HEIRS

Miscellaneous Information

Original documents that are valuable or irreplaceable should be kept in a safe-deposit box, and copies kept in your files.

DOCUMENT Check List #1

☐ Birth Certificates

☐ Death Certificates

☐ Marriage Certificates

☐ Change of Name Certificates

☐ Divorce Decrees or Judgments

☐ Annulment Decrees or Judgments

☐ Adoption Papers

☐ Naturalization Papers

☐ Other _____

_____

_____

DOCUMENT Check List #2

☐ Educational Certificates

☐ Educational Transcripts

☐ Organization Membership Certificates

☐ Organization Awards

☐ Civic Awards

☐ Newspaper Articles

☐ Athletic Awards

☐ Dramatic Awards

☐ Other _____

_____

_____

Original documents that are valuable or irreplaceable should be kept in a safe-deposit box, and copies kept in your files.

DOCUMENT Check List #3

☐ Life Insurance Policies

☐ Medical and Health Insurance Policies

☐ Residence Insurance Policies

☐ Automobile Insurance Policies

☐ Keogh Plan Agreements

☐ I.R.A. Agreements

☐ Other _____

_____

_____

DOCUMENT Check List #4

☐ Social Security Card

☐ Medicare Card

☐ Military Separation Papers

☐ Military Awards

☐ Pension Agreements

☐ Other _____

_____

_____

Original documents that are valuable or irreplaceable should be kept in a safe-deposit box, and copies kept in your files.

DOCUMENT Check List #5

☐ Savings Account Books
☐ Safe-Deposit Box Key
☐ Credit Union Account Books
☐ Other _____

_____

_____

DOCUMENT Check List #6

☐ Stockbroker Account Number
☐ Copies of Deeds
☐ Copies of Leases
☐ Mortgages
☐ Automobile Certificates of Title
☐ Stockbroker Statements
☐ Other _____

_____

_____

Original documents that are valuable or irreplaceable should be kept in a safe-deposit box, and copies kept in your files.

DOCUMENT Check List #7

- ☐ Copy of Will
- ☐ Power of Attorney
- ☐ Copy of Trust Agreement
- ☐ Other _____

  _____

  _____

DOCUMENT Check List #8

- ☐ Funeral Pre-Arrangement Agreement
- ☐ Funeral Pre-Payment Agreement
- ☐ Cemetery Deed
- ☐ Mausoleum Deed
- ☐ Body Bequeathal Papers
- ☐ Uniform Donor Card
- ☐ Other _____

  _____

  _____